W9-BVP-100

From a set of four plates representing the Sculptor, Engraver, Printer, and Painter at work, the first print shows how copperplate engravings are inked, wiped, printed, and dried; the second shows a copperplate etcher and an engraver at their desks, with customers of the printshop in the background.

Bosse followed the methods of Jacques Callot in his etchings and engravings. In more than 1,400 plates he left a record of 17th-century French life, especially of the upper middle class. He is also remembered for his treatise on the methods of copper engraving (Traicté des Manieres de Graver en Taille Douce sur l'Airin) in which these plates appear.

The photographic van used by Roger Fenton during the
Crimean War. This photograph by Roger Fenton,
in 1855, shows his assistant, Marcus Sparling, on the van.
The cumbersome equipment required for photography
in the 1850's made the use of such a van essential for a
photographer like Fenton, who, as a war correspondent,
wished to move about freely to cover war and
war-related scenes during a campaign. LC-USZ62-2319

Viewpoints

4

The photographer in his studio, Iowa City, Iowa. This portrait of Wetherby was made from one of his early glass plates. He had made many portraits in New England before going to Iowa in 1859 and settling in Iowa City. He represents many now almost forgotten photographers who flourished in the small towns in the west as the photographic art spread over the land. Photograph by Isaac Augustus Wetherby [ca 1869]. LC-USZ62-3529.

VIEWPOINTS

A Selection from the Pictorial Collections of the Library of Congress

A Picture Book by Alan Fern, Milton Kaplan, and the Staff of the Prints and Photographs Division

LIBRARY OF CONGRESS   WASHINGTON   1975

Library of Congress Cataloging in Publication Data

United States.   Library of Congress.   Prints and
  Photographs Division.
    Viewpoints: a selection from the pictorial collec-
tions of the Library of Congress.

    Includes bibliographical references.
    1. United States—History—Pictorial works.
2. History, Modern—Pictorial works. 3. United
States. Library of Congress. Prints and Photographs
Division. I. Fern, Alan Maxwell, 1930-
II. Kaplan, Milton, 1918-   III. United States.
Library of Congress. IV. Title.
E178.5.U54   1974   973'.022'2   73-18317
ISBN 0-8444-0113-7

For sale by the Superintendent of Documents, U.S. Government Printing Office
Washington, D.C. 20402 - Price $7.75
Stock Number 3014–00001

In May 1962 the Library of Congress presented an exhibition from its collections of prints and photographs entitled "Viewpoints," assembled to coincide with the annual convention of the Special Libraries Association held in Washington that year. The exhibition indicated the scope of the collections and suggested the desirability of a publication at a later date that would make known to a wider audience the extent and availability of the holdings in the Prints and Photographs Division.

While there are more items in this guide than there were in the exhibition, the title used in 1962 again serves to indicate the various approaches and the broad range of subjects found in the work of printmakers and photographers.

The impact of published reproductions cannot be as great as that of the original works, but they can serve as a guide to the range and kinds of collections available and remind viewers how richly rewarding the total experience of the originals, in their true sizes and colors and tonalities, can be.

Publication of this book at this time also marks the 75th anniversary of the formal commencement of activity in the field of visual arts in the Library. Public exhibitions became possible only after the Library had been moved from its overcrowded quarters in the Capitol to its new building, which was officially put into service November 1, 1897. Before that date, on July 1, a Division of Prints had been established by Congressional authorization. By mid-1898 visitors to the Library were being offered exhibits of items of special interest from the considerable collections of prints already in the Library's custody. By 1901 there had been 30 exhibitions of prints and since that time there has been a continuing series of exhibitions reflecting and illustrating the collections indicated on the pages that follow.

Many members of the Prints and Photographs Division assisted in the selection of the works represented in this book and provided the research upon which the captions are based.

Foreword

The curators and specialists contributed sections on their individual areas of interest, and Milton Kaplan, the division's curator of historical prints, did much of the final writing of this book and devoted himself to searching out many of the examples finally used. Mrs. Jeanne Tifft, who was formerly cataloger of fine prints, wrote many of the captions used in the 1962 exhibition and a number of her ideas have been retained in this publication. Much help was also given by Herbert Sanborn and Arthur Burton of the Library's Exhibits Office, and by the staff of the Library's Publications Office. The task of expanding and editing the book for publication was carried out by William C. Ackerman, an editor in the Publications Office.

Between the time of its conception and the publication of this volume, one of the staff of the Prints and Photographs Division died. Hirst D. Milhollen had devoted more than 40 years to the growth and arrangement of the pictorial collections, as well as to their study and interpretation, and was directly responsible for some of the most significant acquisitions recorded in these pages. His colleagues honor his memory through their work on this publication, which stands as a tangible expression of the values Hirst Milhollen did so much to establish.

Edgar Breitenbach, *Chief*
Prints and Photographs Division

June 1973

Contents

Cover for L'Estampe Originale. *The entertainer Jane Avril is portrayed inspecting a freshly printed sheet at the lithographic printing shop of Ancourt, where many of Toulouse-Lautrec's lithographs were printed. Père Cotelle, the most skilled pressman at Ancourt's, is shown working the hand press. Color lithograph by Henri de Toulouse-Lautrec. 1893. Pennell Collection. LC-USZ62-17348.*

Pictorial materials have had a place in the Library of Congress from its very earliest days. Apart from illustrated books, pictures on separate sheets came into the collections in many ways: through gift or purchase, through transfer from other government agencies, and through deposit for copyright. Under the first United States copyright law (1790), and until 1870, copyright registrations were made in local U.S. district courts. One engraving—an unfinished proof of a copy of the Declaration of Independence surrounded by the seals of the original States, and deposited for copyright November 4, 1818, in the Federal Court for the Eastern District of Pennsylvania—is the Library's earliest surviving pictorial item registered for copyright. The administration of copyright was centralized in the Library by legislation in 1870 and the collections that had accumulated in the courts and other agencies, and had not been transferred to the Library earlier, were placed in its custody.*

This centralization of copyright activities in the Library in 1870 and the consequent steady enlargement of the Library's collections has worked, as intended, to the long-term advantage of the Congress and the Nation. The act of Congress could be credited, three-quarters of a century later, with seeking to assure that "henceforth the complete product of the American mind should be treasured up, so far as the copyright system could possibly effect this end . . ." and also with seeking to "put the Library of Congress forever upon a uniquely national basis . . ." (David C. Mearns, *The Story Up to Now: The Library of Congress 1800-1946,* 1947)

Introduction

---

* In administering copyright, Federal courts in the various districts had accumulated considerable collections of the materials which had been entered there for copyright. Reserve collections had also been established, first with the Department of State, later with the Department of the Interior. Nonetheless, in these successive transfers, many pictorial items have been lost, and the surviving deposits must be only a fraction of the original number.

In 1870, with this major new growth factor beginning to work, the Library occupied only rooms in the Capitol; it was severely limited in space yet constantly adding to its collections and expanding its interests. By the 1880's books, prints, maps, and journals were piled everywhere in the cramped rooms, and readers had to squeeze by heaps of books and papers to reach their chairs.

A new building was clearly indicated, and in 1897 it was completed. All the contents of the Library in the Capitol were first transferred to the ground floor of the newly completed building for preliminary classification.

As order emerged, it became obvious that the collections of such special materials as prints and photographs had grown to sizable proportions that would require greater provision than had been made for them, especially if they were to serve as reference and other learning resources in the same way that books had long been used and thus made a part of the Library's basic general service.

This was the course the Library's development was to take. When the functions to be carried out in the new building were being planned, the eminent librarian Melvil Dewey was an expert witness. At hearings before the Joint Committee on the Library in 1896 Mr. Dewey, at that time secretary of the University of the State of New York and director of the State Lirary of the State of New York, was asked if he thought "any attention" ought to be given to the collection of a "fine art exhibition or exhibit" in connection with the new library.

"I do, very decidedly," Dewey said. "The feeling is general among the best educational thinkers of the country that we have got to educate the people *through the eye, not only by reading the conventional language as printed in books, but also the natural language as shown in works of art* and objects of scientific or historical interest. We are outgrowing the curious notion so ingrained in many people that education is something to be had only from the printed page . . ." [Italics added] (U.S. Congress. Senate. Joint Committee on the Library, *The Condition of the Library of Congress,* 1897)

With the expanded opportunities offered by the new building, the Library was soon embarked on broadening the scope of its cultural resources, and in 1898 accepted a major gift of more than 2,700 prints and other pictorial materials, the Gardiner Greene Hubbard Collection. The Library acquired not only a distinguished group of engravings and other old prints but also an important collection relating to Napoleon and including cartoons and posters, and

6

Old Congressional Library in the U.S. Capitol.
Photograph by James E. Wilkins. 1897. LC-USZ62-1819.

7, above

Material removed from the Capitol and deposited in the north basement hall (now occupied by the Music Division) of the main building, the first separate home of the Library of Congress. Photograph by Levin Corbin Handy. [1897?]. LC-USZ62-38244.

8, below

Copyright deposits in the basement of the new Library of Congress building before being classified. Photograph. [1898?]. LC-USZ62-38245.

subsequently a cash endowment. The Hubbard bequest provided the impetus for the establishment of a gallery and the position of gallery supervisor to care for these prints and for others that might be added. Accordingly, space was set aside, and the organization of the Library's print collections began in the first decade of this century. At the beginning, a few of the prints were put in the southeast attic of the Library, but the Librarian reported that in the first year of operation of the new building the greatest number ". . . . remained still on the floors or in packing cases."

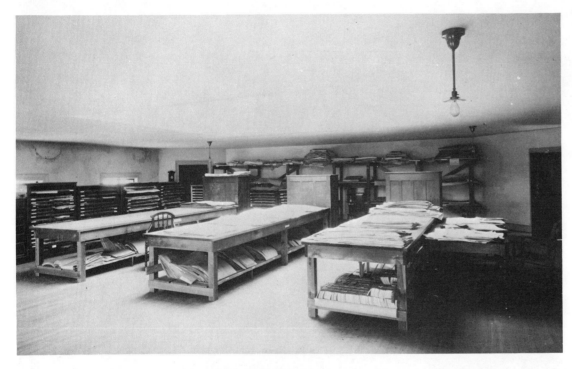

9

First quarters in the new Library of Congress building for storing prints (Southeast pavilion attic). Photograph by Levin Corbin Handy [1898?]. LC-USZ62-38246.

Much progress was soon to follow. By 1905 no prints were on the floor, and none remained in packing cases for long, but to accommodate them the original gallery space had to be filled with specially constructed cases. Other gallery space was established, and a spacious reading room and office were set up in the southeast corner of the Library's second floor—space which was used until 1971 by the Prints and Photographs Division.

Since World War II the collections of pictures have grown to nearly 10 million items, and a large area in the Annex of the Library houses the division's staff and holdings. Thomas

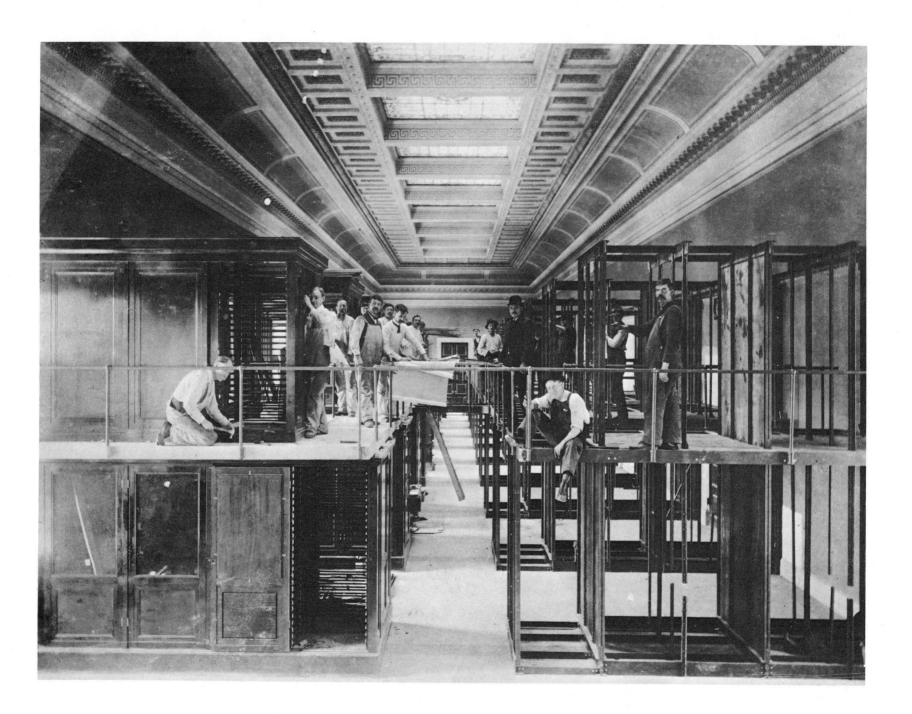

G. Alvord, Jr., the first superintendent of the Art Gallery, could hardly have envisioned that more than 50,000 titles of motion pictures, ranging from short educational films and television commercials to full-length feature entertainment productions, would be included in the collections; nor could he have conceived the extensive development of the collection of original drawings, now one of the most valuable assets of the Prints and Photographs Division. Each successive generation has seen new developments in the scope of the division—which was first the Division of Prints (1897) and then the Division of Fine Arts (1929). In the early 1940's it was realized that the rapidly growing use of the pictorial record made its fullest availability and accessibility of increasing importance for the study and understanding of the past. The decision was accordingly made, in 1944, to change the name of the division to Prints and Photographs, an indication in itself of a major dimension of growth in the Library's picture records and in the scope of its service to the Nation.

This book, issued 75 years after space was first allotted to the pictorial collections, will suggest how varied and rich the resources have become. Many of the collections from which these pictures were taken have been described in *Guide to the Special Collections of Prints and Photographs in the Library of Congress* (Library of Congress, Washington, 1955), compiled by Paul Vanderbilt, and in *American Prints in the Library of Congress: A Catalog of the Collection,* compiled by Karen F. Beall and the staff of the Prints and Photographs Division (and published in 1970 for the Library of Congress by The Johns Hopkins Press); and selected works have been listed or illustrated in the various exhibition catalogs published by the Library. But this is the first publication to present a broad selection of the Library's prints and photographs to represent the world scene as well as the American, and artists of other countries as well as our own.

Many prints required by researchers will be found outside the Prints and Photographs Division. The Rare Book Division, Manuscript Division, Geography and Map Division, Music Division, and the general book collections of the Library are also rich in pictorial materials. In general, however, the Prints and Photographs Division has the primary responsibility for the custody, cataloging, and service of the pictorial holdings of the Library of Congress. Although references are made in the text to such materials in other parts of the Library, all the pictures in this book are from the Prints and Photographs Division's files.

To give some sense of organization to this collection of diverse pictures, several broad

10
Erecting mahogany display cases in the south curtain of the new Library of Congress building. Photograph by Flynn Photo Company [ca. 1905]. LC-USZ62-3865.

topics have been selected around which pictures of varied content and medium have been grouped. Although the selections are arranged chronologically under headings, there has been no attempt to show continuity or trends or to develop broad ideas other than those the headings themselves suggest.

It is a book of sample selections—one intended to show the variety and richness of material on places and people, ranging in themes from disasters to triumphs and in settings from simple objects and occurrences to elaborate scenes and ceremonies. Similarly, the annotations vary from brief lines to longer texts that make it possible to show something of the flow of history that can so often be seen through a single picture(as in *Villa of Brule,* No. 123), or to give added dimensions to the early utilization of a scientific development, i.e. the motion picture (as in the photograph by the American Mutoscope & Biograph Co., No. 177), or to amplify a photograph by an episode in the relation of the photographer and his subject (as in *Pavlova,* No. 181).

These selections largely represent a world preserved for us by the older pictorial arts— before motion pictures, large-page picture magazines, and television recordings. For most of our history it has not been possible to preserve a pictorial record of the times by the multiplicity of means now almost instantaneously available on a worldwide scale. Most of the great pictorial landmarks of the past were more often the products of chance, or of an individual bent on catching in permanent form some evidence of his time, than the results of any organized recording or reporting. They have, therefore, the quality of rarity, and merit the special value we gratefully accord them as links with the past, both at home and abroad, out of which our present has come.

Rarity results, too, from the inherently ephemeral nature of posters, advertisements, broadsides, and playbills. Systematic preservation of such materials has not been a characteristic of these categories, with few, and for the most part, recent, exceptions. As announcements of products and services, such items tend to become outdated and hence superseded and, as claimants on limited space, discarded. Timeliness can give immediate, contemporary value and interest; but timeliness itself cannot last. Hence, items marking a time or an event or a particular purpose soon become obsolete but, at the same time, invaluable to researchers desiring visual access to an earlier period.

In a word, such items are all too often "used up." But, fortunately, there is a legislative preservative that works systematically to help to ensure that graphic materials are collected and maintained: this is the requirement that two copies of each item for copyright must be deposited with the Copyright Office, a department of the Library of Congress. The requirement has not always been fulfilled, nor have all items deposited survived in the collections, but despite some losses a remarkable holding of 19th-century Americana has been created from this source.

It may be significant, in a long-term historical sense, that our modern media are increasingly drawing upon the various forms of older records, bringing significant, often rare, and sometimes unique prints and photographs to television screens, books and magazines, and advertisements. Because such older records are available at the Library of Congress and other institutions, a natural process is at work to give to more people a greater sense of continuities —or at least of what has gone before—that may be relevant to them.

The individual sections of the book, and the selections within them, may provide topics of conversation; any one of the pictures reproduced might have a dozen different attractions for as many individual viewers, or suggest others that might just as well have been included. For example, the lithograph by Henri de Toulouse-Lautrec (No. 5) might interest the historian of printing for its depiction of the lithographic printing press of the 1890's; it might be equally attractive to the student of the theater because it contains a portrait of the entertainer Jane Avril; a lover of the fine arts might see it primarily as a masterful print by a French painter and printmaker of genius and influence; and it might well suggest to some viewers other examples of the artist's work to be seen in the Library's collections.

While annotations may make special mention of a technical development, as for example, chromolithography, the book does not attempt to provide detailed discussions of techniques or extensive definitions of technical terms. Inquiries on chromolithography received by the division are so frequent, however, that it has been necessary to prepare a form statement for distribution. This "Note on Chromolithography" explains that a picture bearing the copyright notice and the name of a firm which published chromolithographs can be assumed to be a chromolithograph and *not* an oil painting. The annotations are intended to add interest to the prints and photographs, but not by any exhaustive, or necessarily consistent, plan of historical summaries or technical comments. This book has been planned to be something like a pleasure trip by airplane over a vast continent, much of it at a high altitude, with only general outlines

11

Frank B. Kellogg being photographed, February 27, 1925. The photograph, showing the equipment of news photographers in the mid-1920's, was made near the White House. Former Ambassador Kellog had been appointed Secretary of State by President Coolidge in the preceding month. Photograph by Herbert E. French. National Photo Company Collection. LC-F81-34548.

visible, but with parts, where landings or longer stops are made, seen in more detail.

It is hoped the annotations will inform the reader, at least briefly, of some of the major collections among those now held by the Library, many bearing the names of their creators or donors, and of some of the particular kinds of material in which the Library is uniquely or at least richly endowed, such as original drawings, photographs, political cartoons, stereographs, and posters.

It is hoped, too, that the contents suggest something of the unending pleasures of discovery and identification of prints and photographs. An outstanding example occurred while this book was in preparation: the acquisition by the Library of a collection of the earliest known photographic images of public buildings in Washington. Attributed to John Plumbe, Jr., "the American Daguerre," these unique daguerreotypes were found, in superb condition, early in 1972 in California. A photograph of the Capitol, probably made in the winter of 1845-46 and before the present cast iron dome was installed, appears with further description and discussion in the section on *Architecture in the United States.*

The works represented are at once documents—telling us how things looked and how men lived in the past—and personal interpretations of the world the artists saw. The photographer as well as the printmaker injects his own feelings and responses into his pictures. Thus, one is invited to speculate, when faced with so many powerful prints and photographs and drawings, about where reality lies: in the subjects or events artists seek to preserve for us, or in the particular insights and impressions they leave for us. One may ask whether the past can ever be separated from the ways in which it has been seen and recorded for us, whether in written or pictorial form? Perhaps this is where some of the fascination of history lies.

Notes

Titles for pictures are transcribed from the originals, with misspellings and punctuation errors corrected. If no title appeared on the picture, a title has been supplied and enclosed in square brackets.

Entries are arranged chronologically by date of production in most cases. Some exceptions have been made in various sections to bring related items more closely together. This is especially the case in the section on Artists' Prints, so that portraits and self-portraits can be grouped together.

To Obtain Photographs

In the absence of copyright or other restrictions, photocopies of the pictures in this publication may be purchased from the Photoduplication Service, Library of Congress, Washington, D.C. 20540. A request should be accompanied by a full description of the item, including the negative number given after the title (and beginning with the designation LC—.) These numbers should be given in full when photocopies are ordered.

Pictures which may be under restrictions, including those arising from a gift to or deposit in the Library of Congress, are indicated by an asterisk after the item number. Information about all such prints or photographs and the names and addresses of those holding the right to give copyright or other permissions, will be furnished by the Prints and Photographs Division on request. This book is published as a guide to the collection of prints and photographs in the Library, and does not give to any user any rights he would not otherwise have to any of the items reproduced here.

World History

The Library's collections of pictures, like its collections of books, maps, and other materials, provide excellent coverage of the foreign scene. It has been the policy of the Prints and Photographs Division to collect pictures about all things that have interested and affected Americans. The result is a pictorial representation of other countries which is about as rich and varied as that of the United States, including architecture, entertainment, agriculture, political personalities, industry, sports, shipping, war, views of cities, and other human interest subjects.

Some of the major collections treating the foreign scene are the Roger Fenton photographs of the Crimean War, the 18th- and 19th-century British political cartoons, World War I and II posters, the E. Crane Chadbourne collection of 19th-century Japanese woodcuts (Yokohama-e) depicting Westerners, the more than 150,000 stereographs that provide a valuable visual record of events and personalities of the period from the 1860's through the 1930's, the collection of 17th- and 18th-century European prints, the Frank G. Carpenter collection of photographs documenting many different aspects of life in many foreign countries during the first quarter of the 20th century, and the extensive personal collection of photographs on the career of Hermann Goering, including his activities as an aviator during World War I and a detailed record of the Nazi years.

In addition to the pictures selected for this section, prints from several of these collections have been reproduced as numbers 1-11 on the endpapers and preceding pages.

Toutes les figures contenues en ce Liure ont este faittes et se vendent à PARIS par
Melchior Tauernier Graueur et Imprimeur du ROY pour les Tailles   Pierre Firens Graueur en Tailles douces demeurant rue
douces, demeurant en Lisle du Palais. sur le Quay à l'Epie d'Or.   St Iaques à l'enseigne de l'Imprimerie en Tailles douces.

12

[LE ROI DONNANT L'ACCOLADE . . .] Etching
and engraving by Abraham Bosse. Published in
Paris by Melchior Tavernier [ca. 1635]

LC-USZ62-22048

One of a series of four plates, it shows ceremonies observed by Louis XIII at the promotion
of Chevaliers of the Order of St. Esprit at Fontainebleau, 1633.

Another example of the work of Abraham
Bosse and of the rare resources in the Gardiner
Greene Hubbard Collection, which represents,
besides French prints, the work of American,
Dutch, English, Flemish, German, and Italian engravers, and some by Danish, Russian, Scandi-
navian, and Spanish artists as well.

Afbeelding van den Brand op 't Tooneel in den Schouwburg te Amsterdam; den 11 den May, 1772.

De vlam barst uit: elk voelt door schrik zich overheeren:
Hoe schielyk kan 't vermaak in jammerklagt verkeeren!
                                                        R.

T. Crajenschot, Excudit.

Representation de l'Incendie du Theatre de la Comedie à Amsterdam; le 11 May, 1772.

La flamme éclate: on fuit; d'effroi le sang se glace:
Qu'en un moment souvent la joye aux pleurs fait place!
                                                        R.

13

REPRÉSENTATION DE L'INCENDIE DU THÉATRE
DE LA COMÉDIE `A AMSTERDAM, LE 11 MAY 1772.
Engraving by C. Bogerts after Pieter Barbiers. T.
Crajenschot, excudit [1772]   LC-USZ62-22043

Dutch and French summaries describe the
fire as it began on the stage of the theatre in Amsterdam on May 11, 1772. Both accounts comment on how rapidly the fire spread and (in the
Dutch) on "how suddenly can enjoyment be
turned into lament!" The hasty exit from the
pit being attempted by the orchestra indicates the
rapid course of the flames.

During the second act of a light opera, set
in a prison, the smell of fire was perceived on
the stage and in the auditorium. The cause quickly
became evident, a Dutch chronicle ·records, "for
when the stage had to be lighted again and, to do
so, the cylinders in which the burning tallows
were standing were opened again, the flame burst
out of one of them. An awkward attempt to put
out the flame failed; the flame burst upward and
ignited the wing to the right. A terrible panic
was created which could not be controlled by
the forceful attempts of the management and
the actors. A great terror was brought on by the
fall of the wing, which came down with a terrific thud, when the ropes were burnt through.
The stage soon was a blaze which quickly spread
into the auditorium. . . .

"People jumped from the boxes and the galleries into the parterre below where safety was
not much greater. . . . The fire was discovered
at 8:30 and already at 9 o'clock the flames burst
high through the roof. . . .

"Meanwhile the fire continued to spread. . . .

In the end two other houses burned down [in
addition to that of Jan Punt, the engraver and
actor], and 20 were damaged. . . . Forty fire units
were on duty, but not much could be saved. . . .
Not until midnight was the fire brought under
control: but at that time the theater had completely burned down.

"Eighteen persons perished in this fire, a
rather small number for a full theater. . . . The
theater was never rebuilt." (H. Brugmans, *Ge-
schiedenis van Amsterdam*, vol. 5, 1931)

Another print, an engraving by Noach van
der Meer, the Younger [1772], shows the fire as it
appeared to a crowd near the *Prinsengracht*, where
"the fire was so fierce that across the canal one
could not stand the glaring heat."

AN OFFERING BEFORE CAPTAIN COOK IN THE SANDWICH ISLANDS. Drawn by J. Webber. The landscape engraved by Middiman, the figures by Hall. Engraving and etching detached from atlas accompanying Captain James Cook and Captain James King, *A Voyage To The Pacific Ocean* . . . London, G. Nicol & T. Cadell, 1784.

LC-USZ62-22035

On a voyage rediscovering the Sandwich Islands (now Hawaii) in 1779 Captain Cook experienced the kind of reception shown, but later lost his life there in a shore scuffle as his landing party was preparing to return to their ships. The third volume of the history of the voyage was written by his associate, Captain James King. Captain Cook named the Islands after his friend and patron Lord Sandwich.

15

COMITÉ DE L'AN DEUXIÈME. Stipple engraving by J. B. Huet, fils [ca. 1793]

LC-USZ62-22047

The powerful Committee of Public Safety, a creation of the French Revolution, was constituted with the same membership from September 1793 to the following July 27, or 9 Thermidor of the Year Two in the parlance of the Revolution (hence, the Committee of the Second Year). The man at the left holds a paper marked "Certificat de Civisme," or good citizenship. Robespierre fell on July 27, 1794, exactly one year to the day after entering the Committee of Public Safety. It was said all 12 members never sat at the green table at one time, some being stationed away from Paris.

COMITÉ DE L'AN DEUXIEME

HODGES EXPLANATION OF A HUNDRED MAGISTRATES.

16

HODGE'S EXPLANATION OF A HUNDRED MAGIS-
TRATES. Etching (hand-colored) by Thomas Row-
landson. 1815.   LC-USZ62-22020

Hodge, "a poor honest country lout, not
overstocked with learning," is questioning the
fairness of the tribunal before which he is appearing. When the chairman asks why Hodge
says it is unfair for him to appear before 100
magistrates rather than the three as shown, he
gets Hodge's whimsical answer that he was taught
in school that "a one and two 0's stood for a
hundred—so, do you see, your Worship be *one,*
and the other two be cyphers!"

The British cartoon collection contains between 9,000 and 10,000 prints, including approximately 2,500 not listed in the *Catalogue of*
Political and Personal Satires, Department of
Prints and Drawings, The British Museum.

17

PURSUIT OF THE FRENCH THROUGH LEIPSIC ON
THE 19TH OCTOBER 1813. "From a drawing made
on the spot." Aquatint (hand-colored). Published
by Robert Bowyer. 1816.   LC-USZ62-22015

This English print is an indication of the
interest that printmakers of one country have
taken in the events of another.

A caption reads: "With a view of the entrance into Richter's Garden through which Bona-
parte made his escape." A decisive battle in the
Napoleonic Wars, it is often called "The Battle
of the Nations" because almost all European nations participated.

18

Lᴇ Jᴀʀᴅɪɴ ᴅᴇꜱ Pʟᴀɴᴛᴇꜱ ᴀ̀ Pᴇᴋɪɴ. Lithograph (hand-colored) by Honoré Daumier. Detached from *Le Charivari,* May 13, 1854.

LC-USZ62-22040

The news that Commodore Perry had opened Japan to Western trade and traffic had an electrifying effect on Europe and the United States. The French caricaturist Daumier imagined the curiosity with which the Western visitor would be greeted and put his idea into this pungent drawing showing a foreign couple displayed as exhibits in the zoo at Peking. Despite the Chinese setting for this caricature, it seems clear that the Japanese situation inspired it. The full caption reads: "The Zoo at Peking; the Chinese admire a quadruped from France and a biped from the same country." The print is one of a number by Daumier which appeared in *Le Charivari* under the heading "Actualités," to designate drawings on news-related or other topical subjects.

19

FIRST LANDING OF AMERICANS IN JAPAN UN-
DER COMMODORE M. C. PERRY AT GORE-HAMA
July 14th, 1853. W. Heine, del. E. Brown, Jr.,
direxit. Lithograph by Sarony & Company. ©1855.
LC-USZ62-3318

One of seven large folio prints (one plate is
a title page) of the expedition. Peter Bernard
William Heine, the official artist of the expedi-
tion, was born in Dresden, Germany, and came to
the United States in 1849. Heine's record of
Perry's trip is also included in Francis L. Hawks'
*Narrative of the Expedition of an American
Squadron to the China Seas and Japan,* 1856.

The print bears a dedication to Commodore
Perry and his officers and men of the "Japan Ex-
pedition," signed by "their obt. Servts. Heine &
Brown."

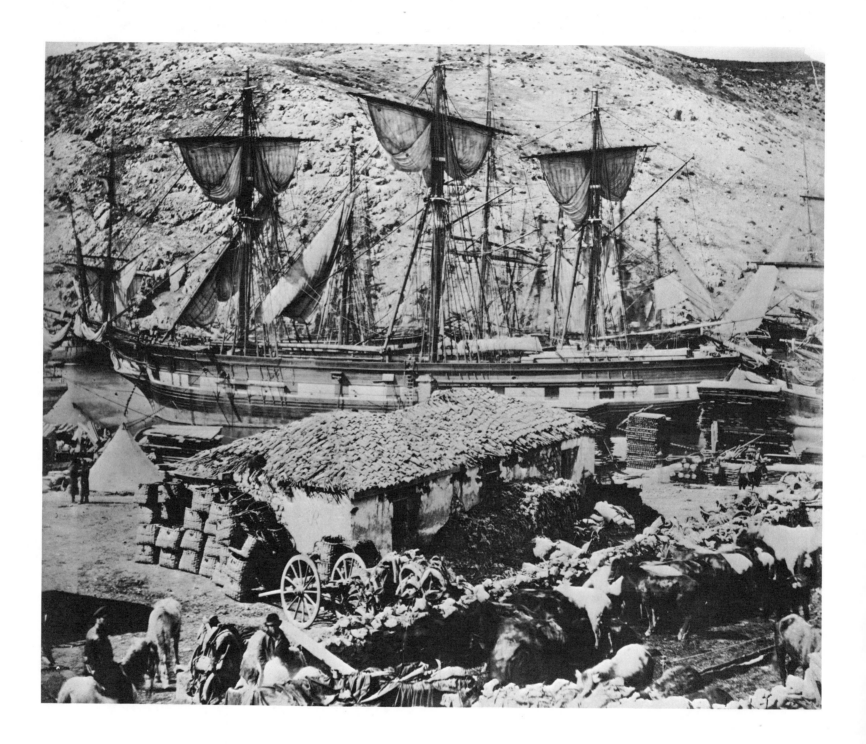

20

BALAKLAVA, THE CASTLE PIER.
LC-USZ62-22030
LIEUTENANT KING, 4TH LIGHT DRAGOONS.
LC-USZ62-22046

Two Crimean War photographs (1855) by the English photographer Roger Fenton are among the first examples of reporting a war. "Though often spoken of as 'the first war photographer' this designation does not, strictly speaking, apply to Fenton . . ." (Helmut Gernsheim in collaboration with Alison Gernsheim, *The History of Photography,* 1955)

Fenton's photographic van (No. 3) was directed more often to scenes, such as the above, which were war related but not actual battle engagements. Fenton's patronage for the enterprise, whether in part governmental as well as by a Manchester publisher, may have been a factor. In any case, ". . . it is clear that it was intended that he should avoid portraying the ravages of war or anything likely to upset people at home; and it is in this light that we have to view Fenton's entire opus of 350-odd Crimean photographs; for herein lies the key to the otherwise puzzling fact that these first war photographs are not very warlike . . ." (Gernsheim)

The collection contains 269 original Fenton photographs, providing an extensive record of scenes related to the war. Of Fenton's work, the London *Times* observed: "The photographer who follows in the wake of modern armies must be content with conditions of repose, and with the still life which remains when the fighting is over, but whatever he represents from the field must be real, and the private soldier has just as good a likeness as the General. Barring faults of manipulation and artistic power, the likenesses must be like, and they must be real if the mechanism is of moderate goodness. When the artist essays to represent motion, he bewilders the plate and makes chaos, and so far as we have yet gone, a photographic 'charge' is an impossibility. Mr. Fenton was probably the first photographer who ever pitched his camera-stand under fire, but Mr. Simpson [William Simpson whose sketches of the Crimean War were lithographed and published by an English firm] was out before him in the Crimea. . . . It was considered something remarkable when Mr. Fenton succeeded in fixing on his plate the puff of smoke from a distant gun." (*American Journal of Photography and the Allied Arts,* October 1, 1862.)

The Division also has the Simpson lithographs referred to above.

21

THE PRINCE OF WALES AND HIS SUITE. October 13, 1860. Half of stereograph taken by Mathew Brady. LC-USZ62-10264

A major event for New York was the visit of the Prince of Wales in 1860, and for Brady's studio his visit to it for "a number of sittings." The studio visitors' book for October 13 was inscribed by "Albert Edward" and other members of his suite. From the left they are (based on identifications in *Harper's Weekly,* November 3, 1860): G. F. Jenner, Dr. Ackland, Captain Grey, General Bruce, Major Teasdale, Lord Lyons (the British Ambassador to the United States during the Civil War), Lord St. Germans, the Prince of Wales, G. D. Engleheart, Duke of Newcastle, Charles G. L. Eliot, Hinchinbrooke, Frederick Warre, William Brodie. (The eldest son of Queen Victoria, the Prince later became King Edward VII, 1901-10.)

In an article on Brady's New Photographic Gallery, at Broadway and 10th Street, *Frank Leslie's Illustrated Newspaper* reported several weeks later (January 5, 1861) details of the Prince's visit: ". . . The Prince visited no other Photographic Gallery, that special honor being reserved for that [Brady's] establishment, acknowledged on all hands to be the first and finest of its kind in America."

Then, in a subjoined account from an unnamed "contemporary," the report continued: "After remaining a short time in the gallery he was taken up to the operating rooms, where, singly and with different members of his suite, he gave the artists a number of sittings. First were taken three imperial groups of the whole party with his Royal Highness as the central figure. Next was executed a full-length photograph of the Prince standing alone. His Royal

Highness had then a number of miniature photographs of himself and the young noblemen of his suite taken singly and in groups, to serve as *cartes des visites*. All the impressions were admirably distinct, the day being peculiarly favorable for the operation, and the members of the royal party to whom the proofs were subsequently shown were loud in their commendations of the accuracy and perfection of the apparatus used in the establishment."

Leslie's concluded: "It need hardly be said that the *éclat* of so distinguished an honor brought the fame of Mr. Brady freshly and prominently before the country, into every section of which accounts of the visit penetrated, or that Brady's Gallery became the 'lion' of fashion and its followers [come] from all parts of the United States."

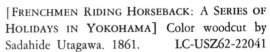

22

[FRENCHMEN RIDING HORSEBACK: A SERIES OF HOLIDAYS IN YOKOHAMA] Color woodcut by Sadahide Utagawa. 1861.   LC-USZ62-22041

The Chadbourne Collection contains 188 nineteenth-century Japanese woodcuts, printed in colors, showing Americans and Europeans and their way of life in Japan, as they appeared to Japanese artists after the opening of the country to foreign trade in 1853. Westerners, other than Netherlands merchant sailors, were virtually unknown in Japan before that time. After Commodore Perry's mission, the Japanese printmakers of Yokohama and Tokyo found a ready market for representations of the foreigner, both in Japan and abroad. These prints introduced Japan to the history of Western invention and technology and showed many aspects of the then largely unknown life outside Japan.

Prints produced before 1853 are generally known as Nagasaki-e, or prints produced at Nagasaki, of which there are six in the Chadbourne Collection, including a plan of Nagasaki in 1801. The collection consists mainly of those known as Yokohama-e, prints produced after 1853, but principally made at Yedo (Tokyo).

GUERRE CIVILE. Lithograph by Édouard Manet. 1871. LC-USZ62-22054

Created by the painter and printmaker Manet, the print marks the Paris Commune which was set up in 1871 to oppose the National Government as too conservative and too ready to accept humiliating peace terms at the end of the Franco-Prussian War. The year saw barricades and bodies in the streets, as depicted by Manet, as well as executions and the burning of the Tuileries Palace and other buildings.

HER MAJESTY QUEEN VICTORIA AT BREAKFAST WITH PRINCESSES BEATRICE AND VICTORIA IN THE 60TH YEAR OF HER REIGN. Stereograph by Underwood & Underwood. © 1897.

LC-USZ62-28242

The only stereograph fully reproduced (the others are only half stereographs) illustrates the principle that two slightly different photographs of the same subject, made by the use of two lenses spaced the same distance apart as human eyes, can produce a third-dimensional image when viewed together through a stereoscopic apparatus.

In the essay "The Stereoscope and the Stereograph" (*The Atlantic Monthly,* June 1859), Oliver Wendell Holmes wrote: "The first effect of looking at a good photograph through the stereoscope is a surprise such as no painting ever produced. The mind feels its way into the very depths of the picture. The scraggy branches of a tree in the foreground run out at us as if they would scratch our eyes out. The elbow of a figure stands forth so as to make us almost uncomfortable . . . A painter shows us masses; the stereoscopic figure spares us nothing, all must be there, every stick, straw, scratch. . . .

"The very things which an artist would leave out, or render imperfectly, the photograph takes infinite care with and so makes its illusions perfect. . . .

". . . [There] will soon be such an enormous collection of forms [stereographs] that they will have to be classified and arranged in vast libraries, as books are now."

The Prints & Photographs Division has such a collection of stereographs. It numbers approximately 150,000 and covers the period from the 1860's to the 1930's, providing excellent pictorial documentation of such varied categories as men,

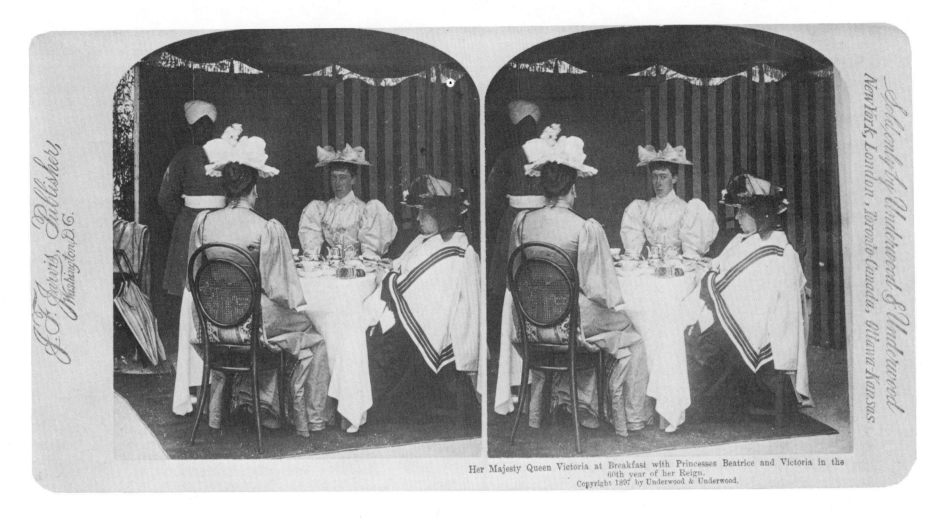

Her Majesty Queen Victoria at Breakfast with Princesses Beatrice and Victoria in the 60th year of her Reign.
Copyright 1897 by Underwood & Underwood.

events, places, war, humor, industry, and transportation, not only in the United States but throughout the world. A stereograph of the kind shown, enabling viewers to see royalty at breakfast, rendered a great service to human curiosity, now served by other media including periodicals and television.

Not only did the stereographs provide many hours of viewing pleasure by bringing the world into the home in three-dimensional pictures, they also had practical uses. Holmes, who invented the inexpensive and popular hand viewer for stereophotographs, wrote: "Already a workman has been traveling about the country with stereographic views of furniture, showing his employer's patterns in this way, and taking orders for them."

The Underwood & Underwood mounts for these stereographs carried the following lines: "Sold only by Underwood & Underwood New York, London, Toronto-Canada, Ottawa-Kansas." The last was apparently a distribution point because of its location on a major railroad.

25

[NAVAL ACTION DURING THE RUSSO-JAPANESE WAR] Half of stereograph by Underwood and Underwood. © 1905.   LC-USZ62-11833

Probably at Port Arthur in 1904, with a Russian cruiser in the foreground, the stereograph records one of many naval engagements in the war. The decisive naval engagement was at Tsushima Straits in 1905. As they passed through the relatively narrow straits, Russian ships that had just made the long voyage from the Baltic came under fire of more modern Japanese ships lying in wait. Admiral Togo, in words reminiscent of Lord Nelson's at Trafalgar a century before, had signaled to all officers and men: "On this one battle rests the fate of our nation. Let every man do his utmost." The major Japanese victory that followed was aided in part by the first use by the Japanese of smokeless powder, a development learned from the French.

26

THE SURRENDER OF JERUSALEM, DECEMBER 9, 1917. Photograph by Hol Lars Larsson.

LC-M32-1831

The Mayor of Jerusalem, Hussein Hashim El-Husseini (with cane), surrenders the city to two sergeants at a British outpost on the Jaffa Road outside the city. This photograph is from the original stereographic negative—the only negative taken of this historic event which signaled the end of 13 centuries of Islamic rule of the Holy City. It is one of 20,000 original negatives (4,000 of which are stereographic) given to the Library in 1966 by G. Eric Matson and his wife Edith. The Matson Collection provides excellent documentation of persons, places, and events in Palestine and the Middle East during their half century of residence in the Holy Land. The emigration of his and several other farming families from Sweden to Jerusalem in 1896 was the subject of Selma Lagerlöf's 1903 Nobel Prize-winning novel *Jerusalem.* There they joined the "American Colony," a small group which had come from the midwestern United States in 1881 to lead a communal life close to that of the early Christians. One of the communal economic enterprises was a photo department, known as the American Colony Photographers, which later became the Matson Photo Service.

27

NIEDER MIT DEN ABTREIBUNGS-PARAGRAPHEN. Lithograph by Käthe Kollwitz. 1924.

LC-USZ62-22028

This poster was published by the Communist Party of Germany ("Herausgegeben von der KPD"—Kommunistische Partei Deutschlands) in opposition to paragraphs of the German Penal Code directed against women who undergo abortions. The bold-face lettering reads: "Down With the Abortion Paragraphs!" The lithographer was married to a physician who practised in a poor section of Berlin, and devoted her intense energy as an artist to depicting with deep sympathy the condition of those who lived around her.

28

NATIONAL SOZIALIST ODER UMSONST WAREN
DIE OPFER. Lithograph by H. Busch. 1928.
LC-USZ62-22055

The picture of a German soldier of World
War I in battle gear and the legend on the poster
convey the effort of the Nazis to appear as heirs
of the ideals for which German soldiers in World
War I had fought. The text of this poster for the
May 20, 1928, Reichstag election translates:
"National Socialist or their sacrifice will have been
in vain."

29

HE'S WATCHING YOU. Color poster published by the United States Division of Information, Office of Emergency Management. 1942.

LC-USZ62-22049

The image in this U.S. poster is perhaps only accidentally similar to that in the German poster reproduced on the facing page.

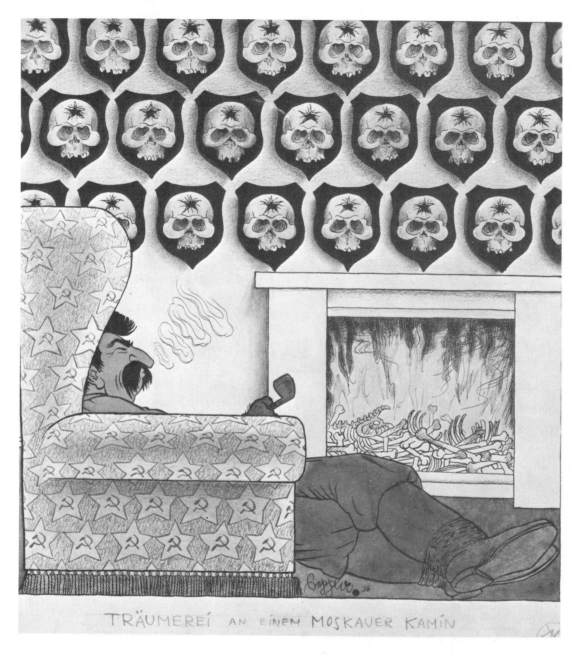

TRÄUMEREI AN EINEM MOSKAUER KAMIN

30

TRÄUMEREI AN EINEM MOSKAUER KAMIN. Ink-and-watercolor drawing, signed Seppla. 1936.

LC-USZ62-22008

Before World War II brought Hitler's Germany and Stalin's Russia into open conflict, signs of political antagonism and distrust had appeared —as this drawing by the German cartoonist Josef (Sepp) Plank suggests. Stalin by this time had consolidated his position and was a target of open attack in the Nazi press. This drawing, for reasons unknown, was apparently not reproduced in 1936 but was used, with several changes, as the cover for the May 3, 1938, issue of *Die Brennessel,* a leading Nazi periodical. The principal variation from this drawing was the substitution of human faces for the skulls shown here, perhaps an editor's suggestion to give more force to the cartoonist's commentary.

Force is also given by the line at the bottom of the drawing: "Träumerei an einem Moskauer Kamin." By this line the dreams of Stalin at a Moscow fireplace were suggested as a contrast to those of children at a French fireplace. *Träumereien an Französischen Kaminen* had long been a popular book of children's stories.

The Library has some 350 of the drawings made by Seppla. They represent the glorification of Nazi hopes and pretensions and include virulent attacks on England, the United States, France, Russia, on the Jews, and on both capitalist and communist systems. Many are of such international political figures as Churchill, Leon Blum, Litvinov, Ramsay MacDonald, Trotsky, and many others. Seppla used strong, vivid colors which add to the vigor of his political cartooning.

31

EUROPE. ALL OUR COLORS TO THE MAST. Color
poster designed by Reyn Dirksen. 1950.

LC-USZ62-22057

In 1950 the Economic Cooperation Administration of the U.S. Government sponsored a
poster competition on the theme "Intra-European
cooperation for a better standard of living," and
the Library acquired the 25 prize-winning entries.
The Dirksen poster won first place.

Transportation

The study of older modes of transportation holds a fascination for many people. The horse cart and sailing ship evoke an era long past, when travel time was reckoned in weeks or months, not minutes or hours. The technological advance has been so rapid in the past century that early developments in railroad trains, automobiles, and airplanes have come to seem almost as remote to our time as oxcarts; once familiar means of transportation, like the streetcar, have virtually given way in American life to other forms of surface and sub-surface travel, as they have in other parts of the world.

The record left by artists and photographers makes it possible to recover with astonishing clarity many aspects of early travel. The extent and condition of roads, accommodations, and vehicles have been recorded in prints and photographs like those reproduced. Surprisingly enough, among the best sources are those not primarily intended to record transportation, such as advertisements for products or genre scenes. In these prints the depiction of the world their sponsors sought to convey was often so factual and so detailed that they give other valuable data and aid for the reconstruction of their time.

32

DEPARTURE OF CHARLES' AND ROBERT'S AEROSTATIC GLOBE FROM THE TUILERIES, PARIS, DECEMBER 1, 1783. Pencil and wash drawing by Antoine François Sergent [Marceau] [1783]
LC-USZ62-8922

Professor J. A. C. Charles and Marie-Noël Robert made man's first free ascent in a hydrogen-filled balloon. They covered 27 miles in a little over two hours. Before their takeoff Professor Charles asked Joseph Montgolfier, whose hot-air balloon had carried man aloft for the first time 10 days before, to release a "trial balloon" to show the wind direction. He said to Montgolfier: "It is for you, monsieur, to show us the way to the skies." Visible in the background is the Louvre.

Among many outstanding collections in the Prints and Photographs Division are the Gaston Tissandier Collection and the Bella C. Landauer Collection of early aeronautica. Consisting of original drawings, prints, and posters, these two groups of pictures cover every aspect of man's early attempts at flight.

33

34

PHOENIX LINE, "SAFETY COACHES." . . . RUN-
NING BETWEEN WASHINGTON AND BALTIMORE.
TIME 5 HOURS. Lithograph (hand-colored) by
Moses Swett. Printed by Endicott & Swett [be-
tween 1830 and 1834]   LC-USZ62-17944

In the early 1830's the Iron Horse was only
just beginning to breathe on the necks of
older modes of travel in some areas. While the
Baltimore-Washington stage-coach line, owned by
Beltzhoover & Co., was still functioning, an
English visitor, Lieutenant Coke, reported the
following on a coach ride between the two cities
in 1832: "The coachman . . . . drove most furi-
ously. . . . Ravines and water-courses, which cut up

the road in countless numbers, were no impedi-
ments; he dashed on at a surprising rate, over
rough stones and tottering bridges that would
have cracked every spring in an English carriage.
. . ." (Raphael Semmes, *Baltimore as Seen by
Visitors 1783-1860,* 1953)

Regarding the coach Lt. Coke rode, Semmes
reports that "the great leather springs from which
the body was suspended were given so much play
that they [the passengers] were pitched about like
a ship in a storm, and Coke was only prevented
from being hurled into the laps of his fellow
travelers . . . by holding on to a broad leather
strap which formed a back rest. . . ."

CLIPPER SHIP "RED JACKET." IN THE ICE OFF
CAPE HORN ON HER PASSAGE FROM AUSTRALIA
TO LIVERPOOL, AUGUST 1854. Lithograph (hand-
colored) by Charles Parsons from a drawing by
J. B. Smith & Son. Published by Nathaniel
Currier. ©1855.   LC-USZ62-13275

This print bears the additional information
that the *Red Jacket* was "built by Geo. Thomas
Esq. at Rockland, Me. 1853, for Messrs. Seacomb
& Taylor, Boston, Mass."

35

A STEAMBOAT RACE ON THE MISSISSIPPI RIVER BETWEEN THE "BALTIC" AND THE "DIANA." Lithograph (hand-colored) by Adam Weingaertner after a painting by George F. Fuller. ©1859.
LC-USZ62-2555

International interest in prints of American life is indicated by corner notes showing "London, Goupil & Co." and "Paris, Goupil & Co." The print also bears, among other designations of those who produced or distributed it, the name of the art dealer and publisher, M. Knoedler of New York.

36

EMIGRANT TRAIN, STRAWBERRY VALLEY, GOING EAST. Photographer unknown. Photograph published by Lawrence & Houseworth. 1866.
LC-USZ62-20359

Strawberry Valley, in the Sierra Nevada Mountains in California, was once a mining area and had sites known as Kentucky Gulch, Rich Gulch, and Whisky Gulch. The area saw both the influx of those seeking gold and other opportunities and the departure of those who elected to move on.

An important photographic record of California and Nevada in the 1860's is the George S. Lawrence and Thomas Houseworth Collection of more than 850 prints. Among the many subjects covered are mining towns, churches, buildings, dwellings, missions, lakes, forests, shipping, street scenes, placer and hydraulic mining, and a fairly extensive survey of San Francisco. Lawrence & Houseworth was a San Francisco firm of opticians, importers of optical, mathematical and "philosophical instruments." spectacles, etc. The firm published stereoscopic and other views. It employed several eminent photographers, including Carleton E. Watkins.

37, 38

Baltic Lloyd. Steam Direct to Stettin . . .
The First Class Iron Steamship Ernst
Moritz Arndt . . . Woodcuts printed by H. D.
Gerdts & Co. [1873]

  English Poster: LC-USZ62-16575
  German Poster: LC-USZ62-38241

These posters for a sailing from New York
to the port of Stettin bear witness to the fact
that transatlantic travel during the 19th century
was more than just a one-way flow of immigrants
to the New World. Americans visiting relatives
in the old country, and settlers displeased with
life in the United States, traveled eastward from
New York and other Atlantic coast ports, even
as the ships in the other direction were crowded
with new immigrants.

The Baltic Lloyd Shipping Line issued its
poster for this March crossing of the steamship
in two languages, evidently hoping to reach
prospective passengers whose first language was
German, and who had an insufficient reading
knowledge of English. Except for the difference
in language, the text of the two posters is the
same; the use of *Fraktur* type in the German
poster represents a further attempt to communi-
cate easily with a German-speaking audience,
which was more familiar with this letter-form
than with the roman type used in the English
poster.

The Library's Rare Book Division has a large
collection of these materials, which are also
known as broadsides or broadsheets, covering a
wide variety of subjects.

Baltischer Lloyd.

Dampfschifffahrt nach

Stettin

Via Havre & Copenhagen.

Das elegant und bequem eingerichtete, eiserne Postdampfschiff

ERNST MORITZ ARNDT,

Capt. **F. DREYER**, geht am

Sonnabend, 29. März 1873,

um 2 Uhr Nachmittags vom Pier 13, North River, mit der

U. S. MAIL

direkt nach Stettin, via Havre und Copenhagen.

FRANKLIN, Capt. E. DEHNICKE, folgt April 19th.

Passagepreise, zahlbar in Gold: Erste Cajüte, $100; Zweite Cajüte, $72; Zwischendeck, $30.

Nähere Auskunft ertheilen

CHAS. RAMMELSBERG & CO., AGENTS, 40 BROADWAY, NEW YORK.

oder

H. D. GERDTS & CO., Printers, 13 Frankfort Street, New York.

39

AMERICAN RAILROAD SCENE. LIGHTNING EX-
PRESS TRAINS LEAVING THE JUNCTION. Color
lithograph by Parsons & Atwater. Printed by
Currier & Ives. ©1874.   LC-USZ62-635

Railroading was one of the topical themes, relating to American growth and progress, which were prominent in the Currier & Ives repertoire. Among the pieces of information the print provides is identification of a "Pullman Palace Drawing Room and Sleeping Car" at the lower right. For the most part the firm specialized in prints for home decoration, which tended to be sentimental in nature and appealing to popular taste.

The business established by Nathaniel Currier in 1835 and, after 1856, continued as Currier & Ives, became the most successful publisher of lithographs in the United States during the 19th century. In the 60-odd years they were in business in New York, they published more than 6,800 prints. Of this total the Prints and Photographs Division has approximately 3,000.

While this firm led its competitors in the 19th century, there were many other publishers of lithographs during that time who, although not as well known as Currier & Ives, produced a sizable quantity of prints which also contribute importantly to pictorial documentation of the kinds of changes that were then taking place in the United States. These firms, some of whose prints are reproduced in this section and elsewhere in this book, generally worked on contract, commissioned by business establishments, institutions, and private individuals to produce pictures of factory buildings, stores, hotels, churches, schools, colleges, city views, and a great variety of other subjects. These prints frequently depict the American past with more veracity than the Currier & Ives lithographs. The fields of advertising (posters, labels, etc.) and other commercial printing (music covers, illustrated envelopes, etc.) are also well represented in the collections as contemporary expressions of life in various periods of our history.

40

TUNNEL NO. 3, WEBER CANYON, UTAH. Photographer unknown [187 - ?] LC-USZ62-16883

An eastbound Union Pacific Freight is heading up Weber Canyon, after passing through Tunnel No. 3. There were four tunnels in all cut through for the route to the meeting at Promontory Point, Utah, and two of them were only three-quarters of a mile apart in Weber Canyon. A report on April 27, 1869, said "Tunnel No. 3 fired its last glycerin blast yesterday. . . Tomorrow evening the first car will probably pass through this 508 feet of tunnel work." On May 10, 1869, the Union Pacific and the Central Pacific met at Promontory Point. The driving of a golden spike symbolized connecting the Missouri River and the Pacific Ocean by rail and completing the nation's first transcontinental railroad.

Histories of Utah record that Brigham Young took a contract with the Union Pacific Railroad Company to construct the grades through Echo and Weber Canyons and westward to Promontory, a distance of 90 miles. He let sub-contracts, and this difficult section of road was built by Mormon settlers.

41

SILVER SPRINGS, FLORIDA. Photograph by George Barker. ©1886. LC-USZ62-17946

A place of tourist and other visitor interest, near Ocala, now seen by electrically driven glass-bottomed boats, Silver Springs has been estimated to be 100,000 years old. The discovery of fossilized remains there is believed to indicate this was a watering place for prehistoric mammals. Barker was especially known for the photographs he took at Niagara Falls, but his views of tropical rivers and vegetation, as in this steamboat landing at Silver Springs, may well have played a role in the developing interest in Florida both as a residence and resort area.

42

THE LAST DEADWOOD [SOUTH DAKOTA] COACH. Photograph by J. C. H. Grabill. ©1890.
LC-USZ62-5073

From 1888 to 1891 John C. H. Grabill of Deadwood, S. Dak., deposited for copyright approximately 100 photographs which he had taken in Colorado, South Dakota, and Wyoming, some of which may have been taken before the last two became states. These photographs, one of the most significant collections of early western Americana in the division, are a record of cattle roundups and branding, railroads, coaches and wagons, Indian life, United States cavalry and infantry, freighting, prospecting, forts and camps, cities and towns, ranchhouses, hunting, mines and smelters, parades, sheepherding, mills, and the "Devil's Tower" geological formation. Grabill left no identifying notes on the valuable documents his camera created, other than brief titles. Other of his photographs are reproduced in the section on "The American Scene."

43

JUNKS, CHINA [189- ?]. Photographer unknown.
LC-USZ62-38243

From 1910 through the early 1920's, Frank G. Carpenter and his daughter, Mrs. W. Chapin Huntington, traveled over much of the world taking and collecting photographs to illustrate their voluminous popular writings on geography. The emphasis throughout the varied Carpenter Collection of approximately 20,000 photographs is on the inhabitants of particular countries or areas and their environments. Of special interest is the large group of 19th-century albumen prints they acquired from various commercial firms operating in the countries they visited.

44

BUFFALO CART, JAVA [189 - ?]. Photographer unknown.   LC-USZ62-38248

45

SEDAN CHAIR, CHINA [189 - ?]. Photographer unknown.   LC-USZ62-38247

These additional photographs from the Carpenter Collection represent the wide range of subjects covered in the collection, a variety that embraces monuments, fakirs, street scenes, cafes and hotels, schools, and many other subjects, from all continents.

46

INTERIOR OF DINING CARS ON THE CINCINNATI, HAMILTON & DAYTON R. R. Color lithograph by the Strobridge Lithographing Company. [©1894]. LC-USZ62-22022

The rider in this dining car did not lack for commercial comforts and conveniences, or at least for reminders of their availability. Labels and signs include Crescent Brewing Co., Joseph R. Peebles' Sons Co. (whisky), "Peebles Perfectos," and, in a page of the *Cincinnati Times-Star,* an ad of the Cook Carriage Co. of Cincinnati. Through the window is the plant of the Mosler Safe Co. of Hamilton, Ohio. A possible conjecture might be whether the cost of publication and distribution of the print may have been shared by the several advertisers whose products are so strongly featured, or whether it might have been sufficient return for the railroad to be so identified with trade and commerce of various kinds.

47

STREET CAR, WASHINGTON, D.C. Photographer
unknown [ca. 1895]   LC-USZ62-15878

The photograph was taken during experiments with a surface contact system, using a skate to supply power at the front of the car, which was owned by Eckington & Soldiers Home Railway Co.

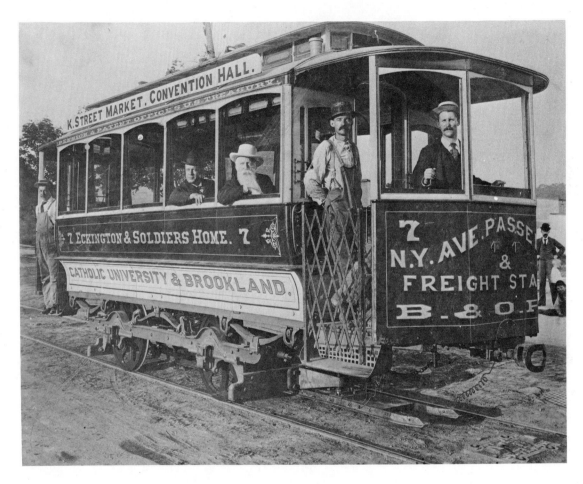

48

SURREY, WHITE HOUSE STABLES, WASHINGTON, D.C. Photograph by Waldon Fawcett. ©1903.
LC-USZ62-19336

This basket-type surrey was Mrs. Theodore Roosevelt's favorite vehicle. The White House stables were then at the rear of what is now the Executive Office Building, which shows in the background, and across from the Corcoran Art Gallery.

President Theodore Roosevelt depended on horse-drawn transportation throughout his administrations. "I came to the inauguration in this horse-drawn vehicle and I will leave in it," he said as he left office in 1909. He did, however, make some use of the automobile when away from his official duties in Washington. (Herbert Ridgeway Collins, *Presidents on Wheels,* 1971)

49

FLIGHT OF THE WRIGHT BROTHERS AT KITTY HAWK, NORTH CAROLINA, DECEMBER 17, 1903. Photograph by Orville Wright and John T. Daniels.
LC-USZ62-6166A

The historic first powered flight was recorded for posterity by Orville Wright, who had rigged a camera with its lens trained on the end of the starting rail so a picture could be made when the airplane left the ground. He can be seen lying in the operator's prone position. His brother Wilbur can be seen running alongside to steady the wing after it left its resting position on the benchlike object in the center foreground. As the plane began to rise into a stiff head wind at 10:35 a.m., John T. Daniels of the Kill Devil Life Saving Station clicked the shutter.

50

Automobiling in the Hills of Southern Vermont. Photograph (half of a stereograph) by H. C. White Company. ©1906. LC-USZ62-28456

The H.C. White Company of Bennington, Vt., was one of a number of firms that produced stereographs covering many different aspects of American life.

51

A Mississippi River Landing. Photograph by the Detroit Publishing Company. ©1906.

LC-D4-19395

An excellent photographic survey of the United States during the first decade of the 20th century is available in the Library's collection of some 20,000 photoprints and 30,000 original glass-plate negatives made by the Detroit Publishing Co., of Detroit, Mich., earlier known as the Detroit Photographic Co. The subjects in the collection include not only large cities (streets, buildings, historic monuments, etc.), but also small towns, rural areas, scenic views, industry, farming, various means of transportation, and sports activities.

All roads lead to SWITZERLAND

52

ALL ROADS LEAD TO SWITZERLAND. Color poster by Herbert Matter [193 -]   LC-USZ62-22053

Modern posters constitute one of the principal collections in the Prints and Photographs Division. More than 50,000 examples have been collected, both from the United States and from many foreign countries. This example from Switzerland is followed by one from England.

53

LONDON TRANSPORT SIGHTSEEING BUS TOURS.
Color poster designed by George Brzezinski Karo
[ca. 1960]   LC-USZ62-22050

Under the design leadership of Frank Pick
and his successors, the London Transport system
has had a uniquely long (since 1908) and distinguished history of commissioning posters from
leading artists to advertise its services and brighten
its stations. The story is told, with many examples, in the London Transport Executive's *Art
for All. London Transport Posters 1908-1949*,
1949.

The raw materials of history are, for most historians, written sources such as contemporary documents, treaties, journals, diaries, letters, newspapers. Pictures, commonly used as illustrations to give an idea of how people or places looked, can also be valuable original documents in themselves.

Paul Revere's engraving of the Boston Massacre was made shortly after the incident took place. Probably the most famous and the most valuable of his prints, the "Boston Massacre" was published at the height of the Revolutionary fervor and, by providing a pictorial record of the episode, gave added impetus to the colonists' cause.

The strong interest taken by the French in the young nation is indicated by the engraving of the riot in New York and by the French copy after John Trumbull's painting of the signing of the Declaration of Independence, now in the U.S. Capitol. The impact of America on Europe is further suggested by the John Dixon mezzotint from the collection of approximately 10,000 British political and social cartoons which cover the period from the early 1700's to the 1850's; the Chodowiecki engravings; the Thornton engraving; and the War of 1812 cartoon. During the latter part of the 18th and well into the 19th centuries a substantial number of prints on American themes were published in Europe. These prints provide one of the important sources for the study of American history, for they frequently offer contemporary pictorial comments on subjects not covered by American prints.

Although the contemporary pictorial record of the American Revolution and the War of 1812 is somewhat sparse, there is a substantial body of pictures of the later wars in which the United States has been engaged, the most comprehensive collections in the Library of Congress being those of the Civil War. These collections include prints by Currier & Ives and by other lithographing firms of the 1860's, original pencil sketches and wash drawings

United States History

made in the field by staff artists of *Harper's Weekly* and of *Frank Leslie's Illustrated Newspaper,* and a magnificent collection of photographs, both original glass-plate negatives and prints.

For the study of the Civil War, including the kinds of commitment to the opposing sides given by their respective adherents, the division also provides a little-known collection of several thousand illustrated envelopes. The illustrations, which usually appear on the front of the envelope in the upper left corner, include small portraits, eagles, flags and other emblems, pictures of military and naval actions, camp scenes, cartoons, views of cities, and slogans or mottoes, often in bright and varied colors. The envelopes came from enterprising printers who sensed that letter-writers in both North and South would be eager to display their sentiments and, perhaps, advance the cause which they supported.

Annotations in this section will refer further to the state of the art of of making pictures for newspapers and magazines in the Civil War years, i.e., field sketches reproduced by the use of woodcuts. But it might be noted that even then techniques were beginning that by the end of the century would make possible the reproduction of photographs by half-tone blocks so they could be printed as illustrations alongside articles in newspapers and other publications. This was to broaden greatly the scope of pictorial reproduction of current history. The key lay in the development of screens, lines, and dots to recreate the tones of a photograph on a printing plate, without resort to copying by hand—the technique of pictorial print media today. There were many contributors from several countries. Fox Talbot of England first explored the use of a mesh or screen in 1852-53. In Canada, as information brought to the attention of photographic historians only a few years ago has disclosed, the *Canadian Illustrated News* of October 30, 1869, was "the first in the world to use halftone reproductions of photographs . . ." These halftones were the work of William Augustus Leggo, a Quebec engraver, who later moved to New York. (Ralph Greenhill, *Early Photography in Canada,* 1965). In 1880 Stephen H. Horgan in the *New York Daily Graphic* used a single-line Leggo screen for his famous "Shantytown, New York," further demonstrating the feasibility of printing a photo-block. George Meisenbach of Munich used a related process three years later. Important contributors to the development of the halftone art in the eighties and nineties were the Americans Frederick E. Ives and

Louis E. and Max Levy. "Yet, surprising as it may seem, development was extremely slow and up to the end of the century, woodcuts copied from photographs or artists' drawings, remained the common form of illustration for weeklies and magazines." (Helmut Gernsheim, in collaboration with Alison Gernsheim, *The History of Photography,* 1969). Although the new century brought more sophisticated technical equipment for the pictorial reporting of U.S. as well as world history, the earlier methods fortunately provide extensive records of Civil War and other 19th-century events that were at least based on photographs or on-the-spot sketches.

Like other documents, most pictorial documents require study and research. Sometimes things are not as they seem to be. We should not accept the ambience some prints possess without knowing the basis on which it rests. During the Spanish-American War, for example, the war correspondents who accompanied the American forces sent back very colorful accounts of the exploits of the Army. W. G. Read's depiction of the charge of the Rough Riders up San Juan Hill, their bugles blowing, banners flying, and horses plunging, was probably just what the public at home came to believe. Although it does not exaggerate the spirit of the men, it is not an accurate portrayal of the event. Because the terrain was unsuitable for horses, the regiment, as Colonel Theodore Roosevelt reported, had left them behind and struggled on foot up the hill. A more accurate depiction of the kind of battle fought at San Juan Hill is given in the William Glackens drawing, "El Pozo," which was reproduced in *McClure's Magazine,* October 1898, with the caption "The Rough Riders Charging up San Juan Hill, July 1st, and Driving the Spanish from their Intrenchments."

It is interesting to speculate why the drawing was presented as San Juan Hill since it is marked El Pozo (actually "El Poso") in the drawing. Reproduced in the same article is a map of the field of operations before Santiago which clearly shows El Pozo and San Juan Hill to be different places. Did an editor change the title on the drawing because San Juan Hill had become the popular name by which the whole operation was being remembered, or did the change result from confusion on his part about the two places, or did he have further information confirming that the action shown was at San Juan Hill and the sketch made later at El Pozo, back of the actual battle area? The "Rough Riders" in the Glackens drawing have dismounted, giving some credence to the view that it may represent San Juan Hill after all. Without pressing the pursuit of a clear identification further—a pursuit in which the collector or user or curator of prints and photographs must often engage—we might leave the suggestion that the hill under assault is one with a building at the top. San Juan or El Pozo?

For the student of the American political scene, there are portraits of political leaders, Presidential campaign banners, photographs and drawings of events in which the men of politics played a part, and an extraordinarily extensive collection of political cartoons which are often as eloquent as essays in revealing the passions that underlay important incidents in the American past.

54

COTTONUS MATHERUS. Mezzotint by Peter Pelham. 1727.   LC-USZ62-22032

Cotton Mather, one of the leading American Puritans of his time, corresponded with several distinguished European scholars and was, as the print notes, a member of the Royal Society of London (Regiae Societatis Londiniensis). He strongly advocated inoculations against smallpox and, in the face of considerable opposition, did much to advance the use of the new weapon against the dreaded disease. In the religious sphere he was also often involved in controversy, including issues that arose in the period of witchcraft trials. This is the first print in the mezzotint process (a technique of tonal engraving devised about 1640 in Germany) to be made in America.

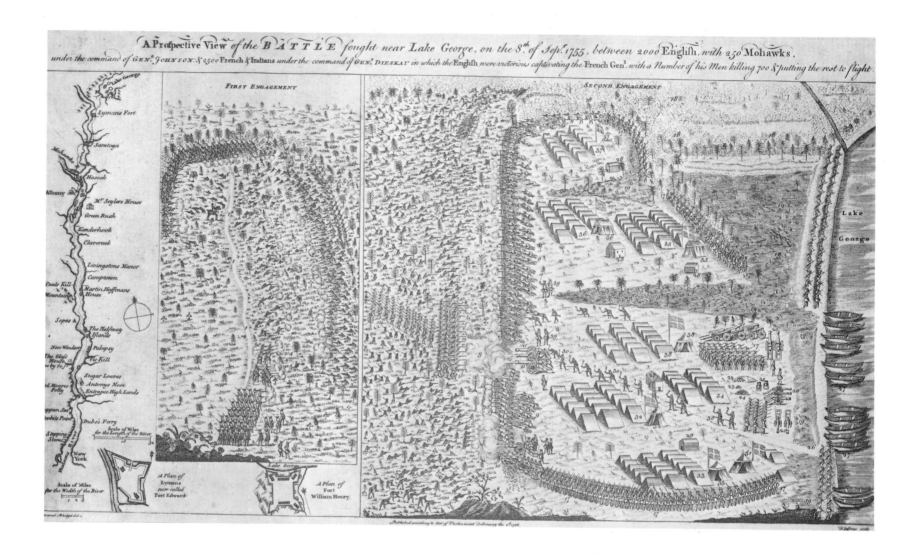

A Prospective View of the BATTLE fought near Lake George, on the 8th of Sepr. 1755, between 2000 English, with 250 Mohawks. under the command of Genl. JOHNSON: & 2500 French & Indians under the command of Genl. DIESKAU in which the English were victorious captivating the French Genl. with a Number of his Men killing 700 & putting the rest to flight.

FIRST ENGAGEMENT

SECOND ENGAGEMENT

A Plan of Lymans now called Fort Edward

A Plan of Fort William Henry.

Lake George

Lake George

Published according to Act of Parliament February the 2d 1756.

55

A Prospective View of the Battle Fought Near Lake George on the 8th of September 1755. Engraving by Thomas Jefferys based on an engraving by Thomas Johnston after a drawing by Samuel Blodget. 1756.   LC-USZ62-22018

This early print bears the line: "Published according to Act of Parliament February the 2d, 1756." The title lines state that the battle was "between 2000 English, with 250 Mohawks, under the command of Genl. Johnson: & 2500 French & Indians under the command of Genl. Dieskau in which the English were victorious *captivating* [italics added] the French Genl. with a number of his men killing 700 & putting the rest to flight."

Blodget's view of the action was described in a 19th-century historian's account: "On the adjacent hill stood one Blodget, who seems to have been a sutler, watching, as well as bushes, trees, and smoke would let him, the progress of the fight, of which he soon after made and published a curious bird's-eye view." (Francis Parkman, *Montcalm and Wolfe,* 1884) Blodget's drawing was engraved by Thomas Johnston and was one of the first engravings, if not the first, of an American historical event. In 1756 it was re-engraved in London by Thomas Jefferys, who later incorporated it in his *A General Topography of North America and the West Indies* (1768).

56

THE BLOODY MASSACRE PERPETRATED IN KING STREET, BOSTON, ON MARCH 5TH, 1770, BY A PART OF THE 29TH REGT. Engraving (hand-colored) by Paul Revere. 1770. LC-USZ62-110

A full account of Revere's engraving of the Boston Massacre and its connection with the Henry Pelham print (which Revere used unabashedly as a model) appears in Clarence S. Brigham, *Paul Revere's Engravings,* 1954. Revere's original copper plate is now in the State House in Boston, in the Archives Office.

The engraving was, in a sense, a news report for many, listing "the unhappy sufferers," five killed and six wounded, "two of them mortally."

The Library has reproduced for sale a facsimile of the Library's own original impression of this historic print, as a part of its observance of the Bicentennial of the American Revolution.

Die Americaner wiedersetzen sich der Stempel Acte, und verbrennen das aus England nach America gesandte Stempel Papier zu Boston. im August 1764.

Die Einwohner von Boston werfen den englisch-ostindischen Thee ins Meer am 18. December 1773.

Das erste Bürger Blut, zu Gründung der Americanischen Freyheit, vergossen bey Lexington am 19ten April 1775.

57

[STAMP ACT RIOT, BOSTON, AUGUST 1764†] Plate 1 (*Date appearing on print. See note below.)   LC-USZ61-449

58

[BOSTON TEA PARTY, DECEMBER 18,† 1773] Plate 2 (*Date appearing on print. See note below.)   LC-USZ61-450

59

[BATTLE OF LEXINGTON, APRIL 19, 1775] Plate 3   LC-USZ62-26669

Three of 12 small etchings by Daniel Berger based on drawings by Daniel Chodowiecki which appeared in Matthias Christian Sprengel's *Allgemeines Historisches Taschenbuch . . . enthaltend für 1784 die Geschichte der Revolution von Nord-America* [1784]

The division has another set of the 12 plates, credited to Chodowiecki as both designer

† Evidence that the titles or legends on historical prints cannot always be accepted as accurate is shown in items 57 and 58. This is especially true of prints made in another country on American historical subjects and done some years after the events themselves.

In the case of item 57 a Stamp Act riot took place in Boston in August 1765, the year the act itself was instituted, not in 1764 as the print states. In item 58 the date of the Boston Tea Party was December 16, instead of December 18, as shown on the print.

and etcher, which differs slightly from the above group.

60

A POLITICAL LESSON. Mezzotint by John Dixon.
1774. LC-USZ62-22038

Dixon, a British artist, is shown as having both drawn and made the print ("invenit et fecit"). The fallen man represents Thomas Gage, the British-appointed governor of Massachusetts. In the summer of 1774, Gage tried to suppress popular opposition to the Boston Port Bill and to strengthen British control of the increasingly rebellious colony by ordering his government removed from Boston to Salem. He ordered the elected assembly dissolved and put into effect the Act for Regulating the Government of Massachusetts, whereby all government officers and judges were appointed by him. Gage tried to arrest the selectmen of Salem but the "gaol keeper" refused to house them. Jurors boycotted the Assizes until the judge told Gage they could not serve under the existing conditions. At the end of August, Gage had to take what was left of his government back to Boston. The broken signpost reads: "To Boston VI Miles," and the standing sign; "To Salem."

J. Dixon invenit et fecit   Published 7 Sepr. 1774.

A POLITICAL LESSON.

LA DESTRUCTION DE LA STATUE ROYALE A NOUVELLE YORCK.

Die Zerstörung der Königlichen Bild
Säule zu Neu Yorck

A Paris chez Basset Rue St Jacques.

La Destruction de la Statue royale
à Nouvelle Yorck

61

LA DESTRUCTION DE LA STATUE ROYALE À NOUVELLE YORCK. Engraving (hand-colored) by André Basset [1776 ?]   LC-USZ62-22023

After the repeal of the Stamp Act in 1766, a leaden equestrian statue of King George III was erected in New York City. At 6 p.m. on July 9, 1776, the Declaration of Independence was read aloud; later that evening the statue was pulled down and melted for bullets.

The Basset print, an entirely fictitious version of the event, is probably based on a print published by François Xavier Habermann in 1776 for use in a "peep show." The use of captions in both French and German indicates a widespread interest in American events, however inaccurately or inadequately they were reported at the time.

62

REPRÉSENTATION DU FEU TERRIBLE À NOUVELLE YORCK. Engraving (hand-colored) by André Basset [1776?]   LC-USZ62-42

One of a series of "peep show" views (hence the reversed title on the top, for correct reading in the mirror of the viewing box) was published in Europe during the 1770's. In addition to this scene of the fire which began September 21, 1776, and destroyed one-quarter of New York, the "peep show" engravers (Basset, Balthazar Frederic Leizelt, and François Xavier Habermann) published prints of Boston, Salem, and Philadelphia which had as little relation to reality as many of the other descriptions of the New World by Europeans who had not seen it. The print itself states that the fire was on September 19.

Lines on the print report the fire almost reached King's College ("Collège du Roi") which became Columbia College and, in a later location, Columbia University. A shifting of the wind has been credited with saving King's College and St. Paul's.

REPRESENTATION DU FEU TERRIBLE A NOUVELLE YORCK.

Représentation du feu terrible à nouvelle Yorck, que les Américains ont allumé pendant la nuit du 19. septembre 1776. par lequel ont été brulés tous les Bâtimens du coté de Vest, a droite de Borse, dans la rue de Broock jusqu'au college du Roi, et plus de 1600. maisons avec l'Eglise de la St. Trinité la Chapelle Luthérienne, et l'école des pauvres.

Paris chez Basset Rue S. Jacques au coin de la rue des Mathurins.

65

Engraved for BARNARD's New Complete & Authentic HISTORY of ENGLAND: A WORK Universally Acknowledged to be the Best Performance of the Kind,—on account of It's Impartiality, Accuracy, New Improve——ments, Superior Elegance, &c.

Hamilton delin.

Thornton sculp.

The SURRENDER of EARL CORNWALLIS (Lieutenant-General of the British Army in North America to GENERAL WASHINGTON & COUNT De ROCHAMBEAU, on the 19th of Oct.r 1781—whereby the P.s of York-Town & Gloucester in Virginia, were then given up to the combined Forces of America & France.

63

THE SURRENDER OF EARL CORNWALLIS . . . TO GENERAL WASHINGTON & COUNT DE ROCHAMBEAU ON THE 19TH OF OCTOBER 1781. Engraving and etching by Thornton based on a drawing by Hamilton, made for Edward Barnard, *The New, Comprehensive and Complete History of England: From the Earliest Period of Authentic Information, to the Middle of the Year MDCCLXXXiii* [1783?]   LC-USZ62-22034

The title caption also contains the following words: ". . . whereby the Posts of York-Town and Gloucester in Virginia were then given up to the combined Forces of America & France."

This is only one of many examples of the way in which the collections of prints and photographs are extended by the book collections in the various divisions of the Library.

64

BATTLE OF LEXINGTON [April 19, 1775] Engraving by Cornelius Tiebout. 1798.
LC-USZ62-13636

Born in New York City during the 1770's, Tiebout was one of the first native American engravers. Apprenticed to a silversmith under whom he learned to engrave, he traveled to London in 1793 to study under the English engraver James Heath, and returned to New York in 1796. Three years later he moved to Philadelphia, and from 1817 to 1824 was a member of the banknote engraving firm of Tanner, Kearney & Tiebout.

A NEW DISPLAY OF THE UNITED STATES. Engraving by Amos Doolittle. 1799. "Printed & sold wholesale by Amos Doolittle." LC-USZ62-1798

"A new display . . ." is the second of three very similar prints Doolittle engraved. The first, entitled "A display of the United States of America," was published in 1791 and featured George Washington surrounded by the arms of the United States and of each of the first 13 States. The third engraving, another "New display. . ." (a portrait of Thomas Jefferson enclosed by a square composed of little squares, each representing a State), was published in 1802.

The slogan at the top of this print is a slight variation of a rallying cry which became popular in U.S. history and grew out of the Franco-American dispute of the late 1790's. France, at war with Great Britain, had been seizing American ships. When a U.S. Commission was sent to Paris in 1797 to work out an agreement about American shipping, it was confronted by a French demand for $250,000 as well as a loan of several million dollars, as proposed by three unofficial agents (the celebrated "X,Y,Z Affair"). The answer was a short negative which has passed into our history as "Millions for defense but not a cent for tribute." The quasi-war with France began, ending with the ratification late in 1801 of a "Convention of Peace, Commerce and Navigation," which had been signed on September 30, 1800.

For each State the engraving gives the number of Senators and Representatives then serving, as well as the total number of "Inhabitants."

In the pamphlet *An Old New Haven Engraver and His Work, Amos Doolittle,* by Rev. William A. Beardsley [1914?], the following comment appears: "We are told that Doolittle was

THE FALL of WASHINGTON or Maddy in full flight.

entirely self-taught as an engraver. This is charitable, for there is no use in incriminating anyone else." To modern eyes, Doolittle's work has considerable vigor and directness, and he is generally considered to be one of the important early American engravers.

66

THE FALL OF WASHINGTON, OR MADDY IN FULL FLIGHT. Etching (hand-colored). Published by S. W. Fores. 1814. LC-USZ62-1559

Published in Piccadilly, London, the print gives an English view of an event in the War of 1812, during President James Madison's first term. In August 1814, the British invaded the Chesapeake Bay and, after defeating the Americans at Bladensburg, Md., marched on Washington on the 24th. Madison and the members of his Cabinet, who had been invited to dinner at the President's House (as the White House was called during the early years of the 19th century), had to flee the city before eating to avoid being captured. [Note comment attributed to Madison about the "best Cabinet supper I ever order'd . . ." and the piece of paper on the ground which reads "Bill of fare for the Cabinet supper at President Maddy's . . . August 24, 1814."] Within a few hours the city was lit up by fires which the British had set to the Capitol, the President's House, and other public buildings.

HBM *Frigate* Macedonian *Capt Carden striking her colours to the* US *Frigate* United States *Com^r Decatur the 25th Octr 1812. Painted from a drawing onboard.*

67

HBM Frigate Macedonian, Capt. Carden, Striking Her Colours to the U.S. Frigate United States, Com'd. Decatur the 25th Octr., 1812. Painted from a Drawing on Board. Engraving by J.Y. [probably Joseph Yeager] 1817.   LC-USZ62-19208

The print was published by P. H. Hansell, Carver and Gilder, Philadelphia.

68

Déclaration de L'Indépendance des États-unis d'Amérique. Engraving by Jean-Pierre-Marie Jazet after the painting by John Trumbull [182 - ?]   LC-USZ62-17349

Most recorded engravings of the Trumbull painting are by American engravers. This one was executed by a French artist, who produced at least 175 different prints, the majority dealing with European historical themes.

The French text under the print reported the event as follows: "When the King of England, George III, weighed down his colonies in America with taxes and vexations, these revolted together, and in diverse actions which the undisciplined patriots kept up against the English Armies, they obtained brilliant successes. In order to reanimate the courage of the Colonists, B. Franklin, J. Adams and several other representatives proposed a plan for a republic and on July 4, 1776, the national Congress promulgated the declaration of Independence of the 13 provinces, an act which was not recognized by England until 1783 after a stubborn war."

DÉCLARATION DE L'INDÉPENDANCE DES ÉTATS-UNIS D'AMÉRIQUE,
le 4 Juillet 1776

71

69

BATTLE OF BUENA VISTA. VIEW OF THE
BATTLE-GROUND AND BATTLE OF "THE ANGOS-
TURA" FOUGHT NEAR BUENA VISTA, MEXICO,
FEBRUARY 23RD, 1847. (LOOKING S. WEST).
From a sketch taken on the spot by Major Eaton,
Aide de Camp to Gen'l. Taylor. Color lithograph
by Henry R. Robinson. ©1847.   LC-USZ62-131

The battle, against General Santa Anna's
forces, was a success for General Zachary Taylor
and contributed to his position as a military hero.
Two years later he was inaugurated President.

BATTLE OF BUENA VISTA.

VIEW OF THE BATTLE GROUND AND BATTLE OF "THE ANGOSTURA" FOUGHT NEAR BUENA VISTA, MEXICO FEBRUARY 23RD 1847. (LOOKING S. WEST.)

70

THE U.S. NAVAL BATTERY DURING THE BOM-
BARDMENT OF VERZ CRUZ ON THE 24 AND 25
OF MARCH 1847. THE BATTERY WAS COMPOSED
OF HEAVY GUNS FROM THE U.S. SQUADRON
UNDER COM'ORE M. C. PERRY AND COMMANDED
BY THE OFFICERS IN THE FOLLOWING ORDER
OPPOSITE THEIR RESPECTIVE GUNS. Painted by
H. Walke, Lt. U. S. N. Drawn on stone by
Pfau. Lithograph (hand-colored) by Sarony &
Major. ©1848.   LC-USZ62-128

The print is the last plate in a series of eight
lithographs entitled "Naval Portfolio. Naval scenes
in the Mexican War by H. Walke, Lieut. U.S.
Navy," probably the finest pictorial record of the
war. During the Mexican War, Henry Walke
served as executive on the bomb-brig VESUVIUS,
and in the Civil War he saw action on the Mississippi River. In 1877 Walke published *Naval
Scenes and Reminiscences of the Civil War in the
United States, on the Southern and Western
Waters During the Years 1861, 1862 and
1863*, which was illustrated with 27 of his own
excellent pictures of naval operations during the
war.

The guns in this print are listed by the
following names: St. Mary's, Albany, Mississippi
(all of 68 lbs) and Potomac (2) and Raritan
(of 32 lbs).

71

GRAND, NATIONAL, WHIG BANNER. PRESS
ONWARD. Lithograph (hand colored) by Nathaniel Currier. ©1848.   LC-USZ62-7554

The forerunner of the large billboard poster
used in later Presidential campaigns was the
one-sheet pictorial banner, a small, highly dec-
orated, hand-colored print.

"Z. Taylor [and] M. Fillmore. The People's
Choice for President & Vice President from 1849
to 1853" were elected, but General Taylor died
in office in 1850.

72

STEPHEN ARNOLD DOUGLAS. Daguerreotype taken in Mathew B. Brady's studio [about 1852] LC-USZ62-1754

An interesting feature of the daguerreotype is that it reverses the image. What appears to be the right side is actually the left. To see Douglas, who achieved fame as "The Little Giant" and Lincoln's contestant in the Lincoln-Douglas debates, as he actually looked, it would be necessary to print the photograph in reverse, since the image in this process is directly on a silver-coated copper plate, and is therefore, under the laws of optics, reversed. The later use of film and glass-plate negatives made it possible to correct the reversed image in the printing, as well as to produce multiple copies.

Some simple tests may be used to distinguish a photograph of a daguerreotype from a photograph made from another photo. The buttons on a male subject's coat may be checked, for example; if the usual direction such a coat is buttoned is reversed, the photo is probably from a daguerreotype (although prisms were sometimes used to make the image appear correctly). A book title or other writing in a daguerreotype will likewise be reversed. An absolute identification cannot be made, however, without examining the original.

The most important early photographic record in the Prints and Photographs Division is the collection of approximately 500 original

daguerreotypes, the majority of them taken in Brady's studio during the 1840's and 1850's. (In 1972 the Library acquired a set of the earliest known daguerreotypes of public buildings in Washington. See No. 142, a view of the Capitol.) Many of the people prominent in government, in the arts, and in the news of the period are represented in the collection, some of the more notable being Jenny Lind, President Franklin Pierce, Winfield Scott, Brigham Young, William Cullen Bryant, Edwin Forrest, and Albert Gallatin, as well as President James K. Polk.

73

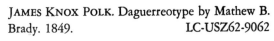

JAMES KNOX POLK. Daguerreotype by Mathew B. Brady. 1849.   LC-USZ62-9062

It is seldom possible to document precisely the day an early photograph was made. One of the few exceptions is this daguerreotype of President Polk. The following appears in an entry in Polk's diary for Wednesday, February 17, 1849: "I yielded to the request of an artist named Brady, of New York, by sitting for my Deguerreotype [sic] likeness today. I sat in the large dining room."

74

THE SECOND BATTLE OF BULL RUN, FOUGHT AUGUST 29TH, 1862 . . . Lithograph (hand-colored) by Currier & Ives [1862]

LC-USZ62-147

In addition to the prints based on drawings made from direct observation, a number of prints were published during the Civil War which are not documents of actual battle scenes but rather pictorial expressions of the feelings of the time. Such a print is Currier & Ives' "The Second Battle of Bull Run," from the Northern view.

The Civil War was uppermost in the minds of the people and there was a market for pictures of all kinds dealing with the war, a market on which Currier & Ives quickly capitalized with rush prints that were merely artists' conceptions. Examination reveals a tremendous similarity between them: a mass of soldiers driving before them another mass of soldiers on a characterless field.

On occasion, the firm moved into the market with a lithograph before the battle had ended. Second Bull Run was not a Union victory, as this print boasts; it was a defeat.

THE SECOND BATTLE OF BULL RUN, FOUGHT AUG.T 29TH 1862.

Between the "Army of Virginia" under Maj.r Gen.l John Pope, and the combined forces of the Rebel Army under Lee, Jackson and others.__ This terrific battle was fought on the identical battle field of Bull run, and lasted with great fury, from daylight until after dark, when the rebels were driven back, and the Union Army rested in triumph on the field.

75

PRESIDENT LINCOLN, GENERAL GEORGE MC-
CLELLAN AND A GROUP OF OFFICERS AT HEAD-
QUARTERS OF THE ARMY OF THE POTOMAC.
Photograph by Alexander Gardner. October 3,
1862.   LC-B8171-7951

After the battle of Antietam, also known as
Sharpsburg, President Lincoln visited General
McClellan at the latter's headquarters near
Harper's Ferry. The original photograph appears
in volume 1 of Gardner's *Photographic Sketch
Book of the War,* published in 1866 by Philp and
Solomon of Washington, and containing, as does
volume 2, 50 original photos. In the text preceding this photo appears the following: "The
evening and night of Thursday and Friday the
President spent at General McClellan's quarters,
occupying much of the time in private conversation with him. In this conversation, it is said,
that when the President alluded to the complaints
that were being made of the slowness of the
General's movements, General McClellan replied,
'You may find those who will go faster than I,
Mr. President, but it is very doubtful if you will
find many who will go further.'"

The best known pictorial record of the Civil
War is the magnificent collection of photographs
taken by Mathew Brady, and his colleagues and
other contemporaries, of whom Alexander Gardner, both as a member of Brady's staff and as an
independent entrepreneur, was one of the principal contributors. Portraits of generals and officers
of lower rank, headquarters, camp scenes, artillery,
railroads, ships, pontoon bridges, towns and
cities, fortifications, and the ruins of war are
some of the subjects covered in the more than
10,000 original glass-plate negatives and prints
available in the division.

THE BATTLE OF STONE RIVER OR MURFREES-
BORO'. REPRESENTING GEN. SAM BEATTY'S
BRIGADE ON THE 31ST OF DECEMBER 1862.
Sketched by A. E. Mathews, 31st Reg. O. V. I.
Lithograph by Middleton Strobridge, & Co.
[1863]   LC-USZ62-143

During the Civil War a relatively small
number of lithographs were based on drawings
made in the field. This print is one of more than
30 scenes based on drawings by Alfred Edward
Mathews, who served in the 31st Ohio, participating in the siege of Corinth and the battles
of Stone River, Lookout Mountain, and Missionary
Ridge. They offer the student of the Civil War
accurate pictures of the scenes portrayed, a
fact attested to in an August 9, 1863, letter from
Major General U.S. Grant to Mathews: ". . . I
have examined the Lithographs of the views taken
by you of the 'Siege of Vicksburg' and do not
hesitate to pronounce them among the most accurate and true to life I have ever seen. They
reflect great credit upon you as a delineator of
landscape views." (Robert Taft, *Artists and Illustrators of the Old West, 1850-1900.* 1953)

The bottom lines of the print give an account by a correspondent for the *Cincinnati Commercial* crediting General Rosecrans with the decisive action which involved Beatty's Brigade.
The lithograph was made in Cincinnati, which
was another of the various major cities in the
United States which produced prints or photographic views in this period.

The Battle of Stone River or Murfreesboro'.

Representing Gen. SAM BEATTY'S Brigade on the 31st of December, 1862.

SKETCHED BY A. E. MATHEWS, 31st REG. O. V. I.

77

ALFRED R. WAUD. July 1863. Photograph by
Timothy H. O'Sullivan or Alexander Gardner.
LC-USZ62-533

Shown sketching at Gettysburg, Alfred R.
Waud was a field artist for *Harper's Weekly*,
as was his brother, William Waud. Some 1,200
original pencil and wash drawings of battle
scenes, encampments, naval engagements, infantry marches, etc., for the years 1861-65, constitute
the "unique and unexcelled" Waud Collection.

The Wauds were cited by *Harper's Weekly*,
June 3, 1865, as being among their artists who
had been "not less busy and scarcely less im-
perilled than the soldiers. The fierce shock, the
heavy tumult, the smoky sway of battle from
side to side, the line, the assault, the victory—
they were part of all and their faithful fingers,
depicting the scenes, have made us a part also."

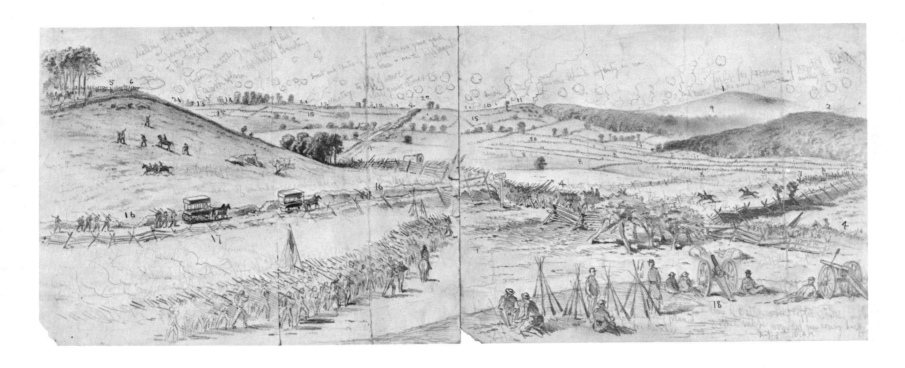

78

The Battle of Gettysburg, July 3, 1863.
Pencil drawing by Edwin Forbes. LC-USZ62-5769

Forbes, a sketch artist for *Frank Leslie's Illustrated Newspaper,* drew this preliminary sketch for a full two-page, highly detailed woodcut, made by a staff artist in New York, that appeared in the issue of July 18, 1863. It was identified as being "From a Sketch by our Special Artist, Edwin Forbes." In light writing above the horizon Forbes gave information for the engraver on field positions, topography, action, etc. The process of reporting and publishing the news by picture—from preliminary sketch to publication in greatly expanded form—took 15 days in this case, but often it took somewhat longer. The woodcuts used in the weeklies, while serving their important function, could not convey the full individuality and artistic values of the drawings, nor could the average publication time be brought below two to three weeks.

The most important graphic record of the Civil War in the Prints and Photographs Division is the collection of approximately 1,500 original pencil sketches and pencil and wash drawings made on the spot by the "sketch artists" for *Harper's* and *Leslie's* weeklies.

79

80

PALMETTO BATTERY, CHARLESTON, SOUTH CAR-
OLINA. Photograph, probably by George S. Cook
[ca. 1863]   LC-B8184-10358

Cook, a resident of Charleston, S.C., had been
employed by Brady in New York. He became
one of the principal photographers of the Confederate side.

The Cook collection of glass-plate negatives
of the Civil War is in the custody of the Valentine
Museum in Richmond, Va.

MORRIS ISLAND, SOUTH CAROLINA. FULL SAP
(A COMPLETED TRENCH TO THE NEXT PARAL-
LEL) [JULY OR AUGUST 1863]. Photograph by
Haas & Peale.   LC-B8178-17

When acquired by the Library of Congress,
the Haas & Peale collection of 44 glass-plate
negatives was housed in what appeared to be
their original wooden boxes. The names "Haas
& Peale" were scratched into the emulsions of
10 of the plates—the only Civil War negatives
the Prints and Photographs Division has received
that are identified in this manner. In one of the
negatives the original cloud image appears, instead of the painted clouds seen on most other
Civil War negatives.

The clarity and vitality of these photographs
gives them a position among the best taken
during the Civil War. An extended search to
establish the identity of "Haas & Peale," as
individuals and as a firm, has not been successful
to date, although records show a "Lt. Philip
Haas" as a "Photographer General Staff" serving
at least part of the time with the New York
Engineers. A detailed account of what is known
about "The Case of the Disappearing Photographers" and their photographs, by Milton Kaplan, appears in the *Quarterly Journal of the Library
of Congress,* January 1967.

81

ROBERT E. LEE. Photograph by J. Vannerson. 1864.   LC-B8172-1

Lee sat early in 1864 in the Main Street studio of Julian Vannerson, a Richmond photographer, for this familiar portrait. Lee did this "at the entreaty of several Richmond women who wanted new pictures of him. A worthy project was involved—a young Virginia sculptor, Edward V. Valentine, then studying in Berlin, was to make a small statue of General Lee, for sale at a Confederate Bazaar that was to be held in Liverpool for the benefit of disabled Confederate veterans. The relations of the Confederacy with Britain might benefit too—there was still hope of recognition—, and Lee lent himself to the undertaking in a mood of finest compliance, though after what urging from Mrs. Lee we do not know. . . . When he dressed himself for the ordeal of the Vannerson photographs, he apparently made a gallant gesture of deference to the committee of Richmond ladies." (Roy Meredith, *The Face of Robert E. Lee in Life and in Legend,* 1947)

Vannerson is believed to have made four views, three of which survive. They were widely circulated, appearing in London newspapers and periodicals, and also published as lithographs and engravings. The statue also took form, but not in time for the Liverpool Bazaar. Whether the 20-inch statue still exists is not known, but photographs made of it in Europe are in existence, and a description appeared in the *London Index,* the organ in England of the Confederate Government, in 1865.

The portrait has "over the years . . . perhaps been the dominant influence on the scores of artists who have sought to recreate Robert E. Lee. . . ." (Meredith).

82

GENERAL GRANT (LEANING OVER BENCH) IN COUNCIL OF WAR AT BETHESDA CHURCH, VIRGINIA. June 2, 1864. Photograph by Timothy H. O'Sullivan. LC-B8171-730

"At daylight on June 2, the headquarters [of Grant] were moved. . . to a camp near Bethesda Church. . . The pews had been carried out of the church and placed in the shade of the trees surrounding it . . . The ubiquitous photographers were promptly on the ground, and they succeeded in taking several fairly good views of the group. . ." (Horace Porter, *Campaigning with Grant,* 1897)

One of a series of three documentary war photographs taken in an unusual setting, this photo shows General Grant leaning over General Meade's shoulder examining a map. Another shows Grant listening to reports; the third is of Grant writing a dispatch.

83

BEFORE PETERSBURG [EXPLOSION OF THE MINE]
AT SUNRISE, July 30, 1864. Pencil drawing
heightened with Chinese white by Alfred R.
Waud. July 30, 1864.   LC-USZ62-176

The "sketch artists"—well exemplified by
Alfred Waud, who covered the activities of the
Army of the Potomac from the first Battle of
Bull Run to Petersburg—were the prime agents
in bringing scenes of the war to Americans
having access to such media as the weekly newspapers. The wood engraving made after the above
drawing was published in *Harper's Weekly,*
August 20, 1864, falling within the usual time-
period of two to three weeks between the making
of the field sketch and publication of the wood-
engraving.

84

A Dead Confederate Soldier, Petersburg, Virginia, April 1865. Photograph attributed to Thomas C. Roche.   LC-B8171-3175

Roche was one of Brady's principal field photographers, being linked with Timothy H. O'Sullivan and Alexander Gardner as the three most prolific field operators. Brady took some photographs of the war itself, perhaps a few dozen, but his eyesight was failing and as director of an organization he was principally occupied with administration, contacts, and financing.

The two guns lying near the soldier are probably Enfield rifle-muskets.

85

Ruins in Richmond, Virginia, May 1865. Photograph possibly by Timothy H. O'Sullivan.   LC-B815-905

The taller figure at the left is seen only in faint and almost ghostly outline because he moved during the exposure, probably only an accidental addition to the atmosphere but one that complements the other stirrings of life against the ruins.

THE SPIRIT OF TWEED IS MIGHTY STILL; "AND EVEN YET YOU DON'T KNOW WHAT YOU ARE GOING TO DO ABOUT IT!" Pen-and-ink drawing by Thomas Nast. 1886.   LC-USZ62-13093

Thomas Nast, considered to be the father of the American political cartoon, is best known for his attacks against William Marcy Tweed (Boss Tweed) that appeared in *Harper's Weekly* during the 1870's and 1880's. In connection with a cartoon that appeared in the August 19, 1871, issue, Tweed is supposed to have commented to some of the members of the Tweed Ring: "Let's stop them d--n pictures! . . . I don't care so much what they write about me . . . my constituents can't read; but d--n it, they can see pictures." (Albert Bigelow Paine, *Th. Nast: His Period and His Pictures,* 1904)

In the fall of 1871 Nast was offered $500,-000 to take a trip abroad to study art and thus remove himself from his range of attack on Tweed. "Well, I don't think I'll do it," Nast said. "I made up my mind not long ago to put some of those fellows behind the bars, *and I'm going to put them there!*" (Paine)

This cartoon was published in the December 18, 1886, issue of *Harper's Weekly,* long after Tweed's death. The drawing is typical of Nast's style of depicting Tweed's appearance, including a large and radiating diamond stickpin, even after Tweed had been sent to prison, as he was three times and where he died in 1878. Nast dressed Tweed in a street suit but gave it lines suggesting the stripes commonly associated with prisoners' uniforms in penal institutions at that time.

BATTLE OF LAS GUÁSIMAS NEAR SANTIAGO, JUNE 24, 1898. THE 9TH AND 10TH COLORED CAVALRY IN SUPPORT OF THE ROUGH RIDERS. Lithograph by Kurz & Allison. ©1898.

LC-USZ62-134

As the first land engagement of the Spanish-American War, the battle (sometimes called the skirmish) of Las Guásimas was a major milestone on the road to Santiago. "The occupation of Las Guásimas and the area beyond, stretching to the fortifications guarding Santiago, was an essential prelude to any large-scale attack on the city." (Frank Freidel, *The Splendid Little War,* 1958)

The engagement was not won solely by successful, if improvised, strategy. The Rough Riders under Lieutenant Colonel Theodore Roosevelt and Colonel Leonard Wood, exposed to enemy fire for the first time after their landing a few days before, and an experienced detachment of dismounted 10th Cavalry Regulars along with other units, were engaged in direct assault on the Spanish positions. A squadron of the 9th Cavalry arrived to reinforce the Rough Riders after the Spanish had fled; the squadron "had hurried up to get into the fight, and was greatly disappointed to find it over." (Theodore Roosevelt, *The Rough Riders,* 1899)

What the lithograph seeks to depict is apparently a peak point in the action when the Rough Riders from one side and Major General Joseph Wheeler's forces from the other joined on the ridge before the blockhouses and other fortifications. "Directly in front of the Tenth Cavalry rose undoubtedly the strongest point in the Spanish position—two lines of shallow trenches strengthened by heavy stone parapets. The moment the advance was ordered, the black troopers of the Tenth Cavalry forged ahead. They

were no braver certainly than any other men in the line, but their better training enabled them to render more valuable services . . ." (Stephen Bonsal, *The Fight for Santiago,* 1899)

88

[ROOSEVELT AND THE ROUGH RIDERS AT SAN JUAN HILL] Chromolithograph by George S. Harris & Son of watercolor by W. G. Read. ©1898   LC-USZ62-135

As noted in the introduction to this section, this print reflects the spirit of the episode but does not conform to the facts of the terrain, that would not have permitted the kind of cavalry action shown.

Both this print and the one below are discussed in the introduction as illustrations of the need to study prints and photographs and their

legends carefully to determine, insofar as possible, their true historical message.

89

EL POZO [or EL POSO?] Wash drawing by William J. Glackens. July 1898.   LC-USZ62-17843

"El Pozo" as the place was named (but "El Poso" as it appears on the drawing) is one of the 25 original Glackens drawings of the Cuban campaign in the collections. The drawing is one

of five by Glackens used as illustrations for a long eyewitness account of the action at and near San Juan Hill, as reported by Stephen Bonsal in *McClure's Magazine* in October 1898.

Glackens was the only artist-reporter employed by *McClure's* to cover the Spanish-American War, an indication of his extraordinary talents as a draftsman and his delight in observation, assets which were to raise his Spanish-American War series above the ordinary level of journalistic sketching.

After the war Glackens concentrated more and more on painting, and became one of "The

Eight," also known as the "Ashcan Painters." The field reporting in Cuba, in which he sought out and sketched many aspects of the campaign, with close attention to atmosphere and mood, was an important preparatory experience for his later career.

"Today the paintings of 'The Eight' still live. Much of the art-loving public is pleased, rather than shocked, by portrayals of familiar life, while it finds it increasingly difficult to accept the sentimental and artificial studies produced by the Academicians against whom Glackens and his associates revolted. The drawings of the Spanish-American War belong to this tradition. Indeed, because they came in a period of Glackens' career when he was turning away from reporting and finding his way as a painter, so they are important documents in American art as well as significant records of a war." (Alan Fern, in *Quarterly Journal of Current Acquisitions,* Library of Congress, December 1962)

This collection is a gift of the artist's son, Ira Glackens.

90

COLONEL THEODORE ROOSEVELT AND THE "ROUGH RIDERS" AT THE TOP OF SAN JUAN HILL AFTER ITS CAPTURE, JULY 1898. Photograph by William Dinwiddie.   LC-USZ62-7626

One of a series of 14 photographs taken by Dinwiddie of the campaign in Cuba, this photo is one of the most familiar of those of Colonel Roosevelt and the colorful group he led.

92

91

Two Ends of the National Table. The Strange Thing is the Heartlessness of the Brute on the Left. Pen-and-ink drawing by Homer Davenport. 1902.   LC-USZ6-765

Davenport was a cartoonist for the *New York Journal,* which carried this cartoon on April 25, 1902. In the giant figure of the "Trust" he created one of the strongest symbols in American political cartooning of the period. That same year President Theodore Roosevelt began his vigorous campaign of "trust-busting." Davenport's graphic attacks were in the same vein of crusading journalism as Nast's anti-Tweed cartoons. The force of his pen is indicated not only in giant figures but also in such details as the elaborate cloth at one end of the table and the worn and torn covering at the other. Davenport often used long, two-line captions, as in this cartoon, the lines sometimes appearing at both the top and bottom of his drawing.

92

Will He Knock It Out? Pen-and-ink drawing by Clifford K. Berryman [1908] LC-USZ62-1963

President Theodore Roosevelt is pictured in the posture, in Berryman's imagination, of confronting the third-term rumor. Berryman's long experience as a Washington cartoonist began with the *Washington Post* and continued, for more than four decades before his death in 1949, with the Washington *Evening Star* (now the *Washington Star-News*). More than 1,600 of his original pen-and-ink cartoons are on file in the division.

The "Teddy Bear" behind Roosevelt became a standard feature of his cartoons of "T.R." It was a Berryman invention which stands with

other popular animal symbols created by famous cartoonists, such as Nast's donkey and elephant. Berryman took the "Teddy Bear" as such a symbol when, during a Mississippi bear hunt in 1902,

President Roosevelt declined to shoot a cub. The image became popular almost immediately.

Berryman received a Pulitzer Prize for cartooning in 1944.

93

CHILDREN IN A PARADE OF SUFFRAGETTES, MAY 1913. Photograph. Photographer unknown. George Grantham Bain Collection.

LC-B2-2684-2

This photo is one of several, recording a woman suffrage parade and pageant on Long Island, New York, which are included in the Bain Collection of some 100,000 glass-plate negatives. Bain, a resident of Washington, D.C., and later of New York, has been credited with organizing the "1st news photograph service in America." (*Who's Who in New York,* 1929) Starting with a news service, he began about 1898 to mail photos along with his news stories, whenever possible, and soon discovered that editors were interested, not only in news photographs but in others that were illustrative of stories (public buildings, statues, farm scenes, city views, etc.) From this beginning "Bain began to put into file a variety of photographs on subjects that editors might be likely to require; then he mailed out daily or weekly consignments of them as a news service. Thus the photographic agency business started. . ." (*New York Times,* May 11, 1953) Through his Bain News Service and Montauk Photo Concern his customers at one time included some 100 newspapers throughout the country.

Another of his pioneering steps was in meeting incoming transatlantic liners before they landed. "His photographers met ships . . . establishing the custom of taking pictures of celebrities returning from visits to Europe." (*New York Herald Tribune,* April 22, 1944)

Even after a fire in 1909, the collection is still very extensive, providing, for example, a comprehensive coverage of news stories of many kinds for the period 1909-25. The range of subjects includes such categories as American personalities, foreign personalities, arts, sports, New York City (politics, celebrations, notable visitors, street scenes, fires, strikes, conventions, etc.), and political and other public events, both foreign and domestic, among many others.

94

THE LATEST SUFFRAGE RECRUIT [WILLIAM JENNINGS BRYAN] Pen-and-ink drawing by Clifford K. Berryman [1915?]   LC-USZ62-9645

Three times the Democratic candidate for President (1896, 1900, 1908), Bryan favored woman suffrage among other reforms. He served as Secretary of State under Woodrow Wilson, but resigned from the post on June 9, 1915. A comparison of the building-top locale with a photograph of the State-War-Navy Building (now the Executive Office Building) to the west of the White House suggests that Berryman used it for his drawing.

96

95

SHADOWS. Etching by Kerr Eby. [n. d.]
LC-USZ62-436

Kerr Eby enlisted in the U.S. Army in 1917 and saw action in France with various artillery regiments. He made sketches and brought them back in 1919, when he returned to his career as one of America's foremost etchers. In 1936 a collection of 28 of his etchings, based on his sketches, notes, and memories, and entitled *War*, was published by the Yale University Press. "*Shadows* employs . . . effects of masses of undifferentiated human beings and sombre *chiaroscuro*. . . ." (Library of Congress, *An Album of American Battle Art 1755-1918*, 1947)

96

YEARS OF DUST. Color poster by Ben Shahn [1936]
LC-USZ62-19225

Done for the Resettlement Administration, later the Farm Security Administration, this lithographic poster reflects Shahn's greater interest in the image than in the medium. A noted painter and printmaker, as well as photographer, he considered "his posters equal in importance to his other work, although none of his posters is an original in the sense that the artist produced it entirely by hand from beginning to end." (Kneeland McNulty, *The Collected Prints of Ben Shahn*, 1967)

97

Boy, Those Republicans are Split. Pencil drawing by Don Hesse. September 1952.

LC-USZ62-17273

The cartoonist's view of the Eisenhower-Stevenson election campaign of 1952 depicts, through the emblem of one party, the problems of both. Don Hesse is an editorial cartoonist for the *St. Louis Globe-Democrat.*

In no section of this book is the contrast between accurate reporting and rosy sentimentalism more pronounced than here. The American scene has naturally inspired printmakers and photographers to develop themes centered around the beauties of the landscape, and the industry and attractiveness of the people: Currier & Ives' lithographs and George Barker's photographic views are two examples of this approach. At the same time, the rapidly expanding young nation began to take stock of itself in the late 19th and early 20th centuries; political and social problems were beginning to engage photographers, reporters, and artists. Lewis Hine, Jacob Riis, and the Farm Security Administration photographic team were among those who brought about an awareness of the evils of child labor, the wretchedness of the slums, and the human misery that follows in the wake of disaster, depressions, or dispossession from poor to sometimes even poorer housing to make way for redevelopment.

Our cities have changed so completely in physical appearance in the past 50 years that often only a little remains of their original buildings or streets. To give a context to the records of buildings shown in the section on Architecture, early views such as the 17th century print of New York (then "Novum Amsterodamum" or New Amsterdam) or William Birch's "Second Street . . . Philadelphia" are invaluable. The examples reproduced are only a few of the very large group of such early views in the Library's collections.

Other extensive groups of materials in the division include portraits of Indian leaders, photographs of Indian and white villages in the Western territories, and records of exploration parties. Many of these pictures show a sensitivity and technical command far beyond that required for mere documentation. Some of those who recorded the nation's expansion were artists and photographers of uncommon perception, possessed of the penetrating eye.

The American Scene

Such men as J.C.H. Grabill and William Henry Jackson belong on the roster of talented American photographers, along with Mathew B. Brady and others as widely known.

From the Library's large collection of Arnold Genthe photographs, two of his views of the San Francisco fire and earthquake are reproduced, along with one from J.B. Moller's outstanding eight-scene panorama of the city after the flames had subsided.

Another aspect of American life is depicted in a lithograph of a steel mill by Joseph Pennell, a major printmaker of the early 20th century. The print is from the nearly complete collection of his works, dealing with, among other subjects, aspects of industry and labor, which he and his wife, Elizabeth Robins Pennell, gave to the Library of Congress.

A major source for the study of the American scene, and for many of the previous sections as well, is the Cabinet of American Illustration, which includes more than 6,000 drawings by such illustrators and cartoonists as Edwin Austin Abbey, Daniel C. Beard, Clifford K. Berryman, Felix Octavius Carr Darley, Arthur Burdett Frost, John Held, Jr., Frederick Coffay Yohn, Rollin Kirby, Thomas Nast, Edward Penfield, and William Allen Rogers. Represented by a Charles Dana Gibson drawing, this collection continues to grow with additions from other artists, including a number who have contributed to the *New Yorker*. The Cabinet covers the period from the mid-19th century to the present and offers a wide variety of pictorial statements on tastes and attitudes.

The commercial art of the 19th century provides another rich source for the study of the American past. Advertisements, tobacco labels, fashion plates, and music covers not only are fascinating in themselves as insights into commercial history but often present a number of other facets or periods of life in America as well. The F. Mahan fashion plate of 1854, for instance, shows several pieces of furniture and other room decor, the Masonic Temple in Philadelphia, and a portrait of Mahan himself, in addition to clothing styles for various ages. The tobacco label for Harris, Beebe & Company's Choice Honey Dew Tobacco is of interest not only for the study of tobacco advertising in America, but also for the view it gives of fashions and recreational activities of young ladies. The music cover for "The New Costume Polka" suggests the impact the new style had on the American scene beginning in the early 1850's. It also depicts a Philadelphia music store in the background.

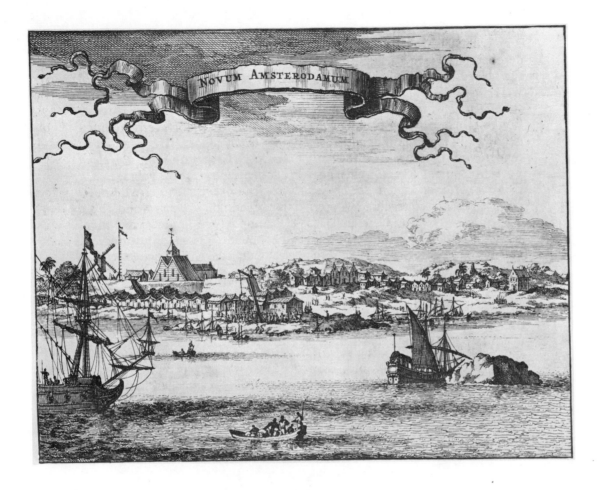

98

NOVUM AMSTERODAMUM. Etching from Arnoldus Montanus, *De Nieuwe en Onbekende Weereld: of Beschrijving van America,* 1671.

LC-USZ62-2287

This plate may have been an adaptation of a wash drawing of 1642 or 1643, which is part of the Phelps Stokes Collection in the New York Public Library and is reproduced in I. N. Phelps Stokes and Daniel C. Haskell's *American His-torical Prints, Early Views of American Cities, Etc.* (1932). Comparison of the two views shows many similarities, including the detail of the church belfry, which was probably just completed shortly before the earlier drawing was made. The general designs of the drawings, down to the decorative banner bearing "Novum Amstero-damum" at the top, are similar, though the banner design in the later drawing is larger and more detailed.

The drawing for this plate may possibly have been made by Augustine Herrman, and be the same one mentioned by Peter Stuyvesant in a letter in 1660. The plate also appears in John Ogilby's *America: Being the Latest, and Most Accurate Description of the New World* (1671).

Drawn & Engraved by W. Birch & Son.

Published by R. Campbell & Co. No. 30 Chesnut Street Philad.ª 1799.

SECOND STREET. North from Market S.^t w.th *CHRIST CHURCH.*

PHILADELPHIA.

99

SECOND STREET, NORTH FROM MARKET STREET, WITH CHRIST CHURCH. PHILADELPHIA. Engraving by William Birch & Son for Birch's *Philadelphia Views*. 1800.   LC-USZ62-3241

Published separately by R. Campbell & Co. in 1799, this view was included in William Russell Birch's *The City of Philadelphia, in the State of Pennsylvania, North America, as it Appeared in the Year 1800*. A few years earlier he had come to Philadelphia from England, where he had become celebrated as a painter of miniatures on enamel, then a popular art in the mother country. He signed himself on some of his Philadelphia engravings as "W. Birch Enamel Painter".

Shown is plate no. 15 in the collation of the first edition, 1800.

100

VIEW OF THE NEW YORK QUARANTINE, STATEN ISLAND. Color aquatint restrike by William James Bennett. ©1833.   LC-USZ62-22014

Although the title gives prominence to the quarantine buildings on Staten Island, the view is of greater importance for the variety of shipping in the harbor.

VIEW OF THE NEW YORK QUARANTINE, STATEN ISLAND.

Published by PARKER & Co. 186, and by LEWIS P. CLOVER, 180 Fulton Street, New York.

During the 1830's William James Bennett produced what is considered to be the finest collection of folio views of American cities and communities in existence. Included are Boston, Troy, N. Y., Richmond, Va., Mobile, Ala., New Orleans, Baltimore, Charleston, S.C., West Point, N. Y., and Washington, D. C. An 1837 announcement of the publisher, Lewis P. Clover, offered prints of the original edition at $4 and $5 each. Their value has increased more than a hundredfold.

A restrike is a print taken from a plate (or woodblock or stone) well after the original work was first created.

101

WA-BAUN-SEE, A POTTAWATOMIE CHIEF.
Lithograph (hand-colored) printed by John T.
Bowen for Thomas L. McKenney & James Hall,
History of the Indian Tribes of North America,
Vol. 2. ©1842.   LC-USZ62-20461

The volumes contain "Biographical Sketches
and Anecdotes of the Principal Chiefs Embellished
With One Hundred Twenty Portraits from the
Indian Gallery of the Department of War, at
Washington." Thomas L. McKenney was "late
of the Indian Department, Washington." Prints
that were "Drawn Printed & Coloured at J. T.
Bowen's Lithographic Establishment" in Philadelphia appear in all three volumes of the set.

Wa-Baun-See was ". . . a warrior of uncommon daring and enterprise, and a chief of great
intelligence and influence." He was "principal
war chief" of the Pottawatomies of the Prairie,
"residing on the Kankakee River, in Illinois . . .

"In the War of 1812 this chief and his tribe
were among the allies of Great Britain and were
engaged in active hostilities against the United
States. But at the treaty held at Greenville, in
1814, he was one of those who, in the Indian
phrase, took the Seventeen Fires by the hand,
and buried the tomahawk. He has ever since been
an undeviating friend of the American government and people." (McKenney & Hall)

TO M^{RS} LYDIA BLOOMER.

THE NEW COSTUME POLKA
COMPOSED
FOR THE PIANO
by
MATHIAS KELLER.

Philadelphia, Lee & Walker, 162 Chesnut S^t.

SUCCESSORS TO GEO. WILLIG.

Plain 25 cts net.
Colored 38

NEW YORK,
Wm HALL & SON.

MEMPHIS TEN.
P. FLAVIO.

NEW ORLEANS.
W^m T MAYO.

102

THE NEW COSTUME POLKA. COMPOSED FOR
THE PIANO BY MATHIAS KELLER. TO MRS.
LYDIA BLOOMER. Lithograph by P. S. Duval
[©1851]   LC-USZ62 2536

The dedication apparently is in error, since
Mrs. Amelia Jenks Bloomer is credited with
popularizing the new style.

Music covers became a chronicle of changing
fashions and customs, celebrities, events, volun-
teer firemen, state militias, Victorian interiors
warmed with coal grates, moonlit rustic arbors—
the whole panorama of scenes about which the
popular songs of the period were written. The
publishers of popular music were among the
principal users of lithography during the 19th
century, because of the appeal that attractive,
illustrated covers had for their products. It has
been said that music-store windows and counters
became "virtual picture galleries of life in America," and with rising sheet-music sales these
pictures moved more and more into the American
home. Music covers are not as widely known as
more standard pictorial sources, yet they often
provide remarkable pictures of people, places, and
things not available elsewhere.

This music cover was available in two prices:

Plain 26 cts. net
Colored 38

PARIS, NEW YORK & PHILADELPHIA FASHIONS FOR SPRING AND SUMMER 1850. PUBLISHED & SOLD BY F. MAHAN, N.º 271 CHESNUT STREET, PHILADELPHIA.

103

THE NEWSBOY. Color lithograph by William E. Winner. ©1853.   LC-USZ62-22042

A box marked "Eagle City Despatch" is mounted on the wall at the side of the door, and the word "Public" appears on a paper the boy holds, perhaps to avoid localization of the scene by the use of a familiar newspaper of a major city. This would have disassociated the print from any of the major cities where print customers might live.

104

PARIS, NEW YORK & PHILADELPHIA FASHIONS FOR SPRING AND SUMMER 1854. PUBLISHED AND SOLD BY F. MAHAN . . . PHILADELPHIA. Lithograph by Peter S. Duval [1854]   LC-USZ62-2612

In addition to backgrounds showing the mode of the time in interior decorating, fashion ads were often set against a view of a new or important building, in this case the exterior of the "new" Masonic Temple in Philadelphia. A similar ad—for the Fall and Winter season of 1899-1900 —was set against the Great Hall of the Library of Congress.

THE LIFE OF A FIREMAN.

The Ruins "Take up" "Man your rope"

NEW YORK, PUBLISHED BY N CURRIER, 152 NASSAU STREET.

105

THE LIFE OF A FIREMAN. THE RUINS. "TAKE UP." "MAN YOUR ROPE." Lithograph (hand-colored) by Louis Maurer. Printed by Nathaniel Currier. ©1854.   LC-USZ62-3330

Unlike many of the more sentimental prints bearing the name of Nathaniel Currier and later of Currier & Ives, this print indicates (as does No. 39) that scenes of urban activity were also prominent in their production. Included in the Library's collection of about 3,000 Currier & Ives prints are views of cities, rural scenes, genre scenes, historical and Biblical stories, sporting events, and portraits of famous people. The firm produced some 30 prints dealing with fires and firefighters.

106

NIAGARA FALLS. Ambrotype [ca. 1854]
LC-USZ62-10208

The ambrotype differs from the daguerreotype in that the image is made on a glass plate rather than on a highly polished metal plate.

Ambrotypes and daguerreotypes were often placed in gilt frames and put into folding cases, some with velvet linings.

107

STAUNTON, VA. Lithograph (hand-colored) printed by Waldemar Rau after drawing by Edward Beyer. ©1857.   LC-USZ62-15357

Almost photographic in its detail, this print of Staunton, done by Beyer is one of many he made of Virginia scenes. This view was separately published but belongs in spirit and style with the 40 color plates in the *Album of Virginia Illustrated by Ed. Beyer,* published in 1858. All of the album prints, like the Staunton view, state in the lower left corner that they were made from nature—the Staunton view using the words "Drawn from Nature by Ed. Beyer," others in the album "Taken from Nature by Ed. Beyer." This note on each print suggests, as does the "Photo from Nature" on the Barnard photograph of the Pinckney Mansion in Charleston, S.C. (in the Architecture section), the desire of the artist to inform his viewers that his presentation was of direct-view images, as he had seen them, not images which were artists' creations.

In the album views Beyer showed a broad range of nature scenes, including rock formations, caves, canals, and tunnels; and the broad scope of resort hotels and communities, many situated at mineral and other springs, and including Hot Springs and White Sulphur Springs. The latter spa was included in the new State of West Virginia in 1863 but at the time of Beyer's album was in Virginia. The album lithographs were produced in Berlin and in Dresden.

110

108

YOSEMITE VALLEY. Photograph by Carleton E. Watkins [1861?]   LC-USZ62-17947

A set of 27 prints of Yosemite in the division was probably taken in 1861 when Watkins made his first photographic trip into the Yosemite valley, using a huge camera of his own construction capable of taking an 18″ x 22″ plate. His photographs of the Yosemite—called in his day Yo Semite—brought him international fame. (Robert Taft, *Photography and the American Scene: A Social History, 1839-1889*, 1938)

109

THE CLIMAX MOWER. THE MOST COMPLETE AND PERFECT MOWER IN THE WORLD. Color lithograph by Louis Maurer. Printed by The Major & Knapp Engraving, Manufacturing & Lithographic Company [ca. 1868]
     LC-USZ62-14084

Another example of the Library's extensive collection of commercial prints, this one is an advertisement for the Corry Machine Co., of Corry, Pennsylvania.

110

HOME WASHING MACHINE & WRINGER. Color lithograph. ©1869.   LC-USZ62-2589

Pictorial records of products for home use that saved both time and labor provide a major source of documentation for the social history of earlier periods. The Library's extensive files of advertisements for commercial products in various periods give special insights into both technological developments and the history of advertising.

111

111

CARSON DESERT, NEVADA. SAND DUNES. Photograph by Timothy H. O'Sullivan for Clarence King, *Geological Exploration of the Fortieth Parallel.* [187-].   LC-USZ62-17356

The King survey (1867) was one of the geological explorations made in the Western part of the United States in the late 1860's and early 1870's which resulted in a large number of photographs of areas then little known to the rest of the country. O'Sullivan, an outstanding photographer of the Civil War on Brady's staff, also explored the Arizona and New Mexico Territories with Lt. George M. Wheeler in 1871-73. Photographs O'Sullivan made are represented in the collections on the West, among them one showing his small boat, containing photographic equipment and a portable darkroom, pulled up in a cove of Black Canyon, on the Colorado River, and suggesting that logistical lessons learned under Brady during the war were proving valuable under other difficult conditions. Also represented in the collections on the West are photographs made by William Henry Jackson for the Ferdinand V. Hayden surveys (U.S. Geological and Geographical Survey of the Territories), including some that were influential in the legislation that established Yellowstone as the first National Park.

112

AMERICAN SCENERY. THE INN ON THE ROAD-
SIDE. Color lithograph by E. Sachse & Company.
©1872.   LC-USZ62-8288

Although his name does not appear on this
print published by a Baltimore firm, the artist
deserves recognition for the amount of detail
the print provides, e.g., houses in the background,
means of transportation, and individuals in various
pursuits. The print is representative of many 19th-
century American lithographs which show scenes
of varied interest and activity.

113

PAYN'S SURE-RAISING FLOUR SOLD HERE. Lithograph by Ferdinand Mayer & Son. ©1873.
LC-USZ62-12436

The falling figures show the openly competitive advertising practices of the time: instead of "Brand X", etc., the "inferior" products bear such labels as "Hecker's Self Raising Flour," "Jewell's Self Leavening," and "Hopkins' Prepared Flour." The figure standing on the table is "Payn's Sure-Raising Flour."

114

HARRIS, BEEBE & COMPANY'S SPECIMEN BRAND CHOICE HONEY DEW TOBACCO. Color lithograph by The Hatch Lithographic Company. ©1874.
LC-USZ62-4633

This print was entered on two occasions for copyright: Oct. 8, 1868, when the company was Harris & Beebe, and April 14, 1874, when the name of the firm was changed to Harris, Beebe & Co. Only the overprinting of the company name was changed.

Dating from a century ago, this advertisement carried a cautionary notice: "The manufacturers of this tobacco have complied with all the requirements of law. Every person is cautioned, under the penalty of law, not to use this package for tobacco again. Sec. 68 Act of July 20, 1868."

The lithograph has the added interest of indicating tastes in dress and outdoor sports of young ladies of the social setting shown.

115

D. ROSENBERG AND SONS STANDARD CARRIAGE VARNISHES. New York. Color lithograph by The Graphic Company. ©1877.   LC-USZ62-14019

A rich source for the study of 19th-century America is the Library's extensive collection of advertising ephemera of the period. Small labels, window posters, and barn-size advertisements not only show the techniques of advertising in the United States but provide a source for the study of many aspects of the social history of the time.

Use of carriages identified with England, France, Russia, and Spain suggests the possibility of export by this firm to overseas markets.

THE GREAT EAST RIVER SUSPENSION BRIDGE.
CONNECTING THE CITIES OF NEW YORK AND
BROOKLYN. FROM NEW YORK LOOKING SOUTH-
EAST. Parsons & Atwater del. Color lithograph
by Currier & Ives. ©1877.   LC-USZ62-420

That pictures often reveal more than the
central subjects being illustrated is indicated
by this lithograph and by the following advertisement. The Great East River Suspension Bridge,
or Brooklyn Bridge, was begun in 1867 and was
formally opened in 1883. It had captured the
imagination of New York, and Currier & Ives
capitalized on this interest. Even before the bridge
was completed they began to publish prints of
it, this one based on the engineer's drawings.
Between 1872 and 1892, the firm issued 19 separate prints of the bridge, nine of them in 1883,
the year of completion.

The Empire Sewing Machine Company featured the bridge in its advertisement below and
thereby equated its product with the tremendous
progress which had been made in the United
States: hand tailoring was being largely superseded, the train would soon completely replace
the stagecoach, and the glorious achievement of
the Brooklyn Bridge, to be the largest suspension
bridge in the world, was taking place.

The print above bears the names of many
working on the bridge, from John E. Roebling,
designer, and Washington S. Roebling, chief engineer, to the superintendent of masonry, general
foreman of laborers, et al. The estimated total
cost of $12 million also appears, as well as the
fact that the bridge was 85 feet wide, "with tracks
for steam cars, roadway for carriages, and walks
for foot passengers. . . ."

THE GREAT EAST RIVER SUSPENSION BRIDGE.
CONNECTING THE CITIES OF NEW YORK & BROOKLYN - FROM NEW YORK LOOKING SOUTH-EAST.

117

EMPIRE SEWING MACHINE COMPANY, NEW
YORK. Color lithograph by Henry Seibert &
Brothers. ©1870.   LC-USZ62-2598

This print features the dimensions of the
bridge ("Total Length from Terminus to Terminus—5,878 feet"), as well as some glimpses of
sewing, past and present. The suggestion has been
made that the threading of steel cable to weave
the supporting strength for the suspension bridge
may have provided further consideration in the
sewing machine company's decision to seek identification with the new bridge through its advertising.

118

NEW YORK AND BROOKLYN BRIDGE. Collotype
by the Albertype Company. ©1889.
                        LC-USZ62-22027

Not only did the printmakers view the Great
East River Suspension Bridge as a theme for
their art, photographers also saw this engineering
feat as a subject for their cameras. The collotype
is a photomechanical process for the making of
reproductions of pictures.

119

A DISPUTED HEAT. CLAIMING A FOUL. Color lithograph by Thomas Worth. Currier & Ives. ©1878. LC-USZ62-22052

A number of hands were frequently involved in the making and issuing of a print such as this one. An extremely busy firm such as Currier & Ives might turn to another for the printing, at the same time securing the copyright for itself. "Printed by Heppenheimer & Maurer" appears, as well as a special credit to one of these partners, i.e. "L. Maurer, lith." It is entirely possible that, while Thomas Worth drew the picture on stone, L. Maurer's credit arose from supervising the printing for his firm.

Nine years later, in 1887, the same print was republished by Currier & Ives, and copyrighted by them, with the title "A Good Race, Well Won."

A DISPUTED HEAT.
CLAIMING A FOUL.

120

NIAGARA FALLS FROM THE CAVE OF THE WINDS.
Photograph by George Barker. ©1886.

LC-USZ62-17945

With his home and headquarters at the falls,
Barker came to national attention because of
his photographs of the falls, rapids, and other
scenes from many vantage points, some dangerous
or at least difficult.

121

LAWN TENNIS. Color lithograph by L. Prang & Company after drawing by Henry Sandham, 1886. ©1887.   LC-USZ62-1244

Louis Prang, whose firm was in Boston, had practiced the trade of his father, a calico printer, in Breslau until he left Europe for the United States at the time of the Revolution of 1848. In Boston he learned wood engraving and lithography and, after the Civil War, began printing chromolithographs. He also began to issue color reproductions of famous paintings and is credited with introducing the Christmas card in the United States during the 1870's.

122

A VEGETABLE STAND IN THE MULBERRY STREET BEND, NEW YORK. Photograph by Jacob August Riis [ca. 1890].   LC-USZ62-11034

As a young police reporter for the *New York Tribune* and later the *New York Evening Sun,* Riis, a Danish immigrant, pioneered in using the camera. His camera and pen produced memorable records of slum conditions in Mulberry Street Bend, as well as at other points in New York City. "Perhaps nothing in all his victorious career so overjoyed him as the wiping out of Mulberry Bend, the worst tenement block in the city, and the building in its place of Mulberry Bend Park and his own Jacob A. Riis Neighborhood House." (*Dictionary of American Biography*)

Riis was not reluctant to admit that learning the art of photography had taken him through some trying times, including the usual process of trial and error. Photographs were reproduced only from drawings based on the photographs. In an article by Riis entitled "How the Other Half Lives: Studies Among the Tenements" (*Scribner's Magazine, December* 1899), 19 drawings made "after the author's instantaneous photographs," according to an editorial note, were used as illustrations of the conditions he had observed.

Only recently has the photographic quality of Riis's work come to be appreciated. Citing Riis as "America's first journalist-photographer," *U.S. Camera 1948* presented selections from a set of his prints (on "The Battle With the Slum") as being "probably the first as well as one of the greatest sets of documentary pictures produced in the hundred plus years of American photo history." (See also article by J. Riis Owre, a grandson and educator, in *The American-Scandinavian Review,* March 1967.)

VILLA OF BRULE. THE GREAT HOSTILE INDIAN
CAMP ON RIVER BRULE NEAR PINE RIDGE,
SOUTH DAKOTA. Photograph by John C. H. Gra-
bill. © 1891.   LC-USZ62-19725

A photograph or print can portray a single, isolated event or it can, as in this example, suggest the flow of history. The disarmingly peaceful scene pictured here actually lay close, in both time and place, to a succession of climactic events, culminating in the final days of the Sioux as a nation. With the sturdy survival of descendants—and of long-running problems the American Indian has faced for a century and more—some of the history suggested by this photograph has come down to our own day.

Grabill left some of the finest photographs of various phases of late frontier life but, by providing only brief captions, also left problems of identification. The significance he saw in the cryptic "Villa of Brule" title, as reproduced above, has not been ascertained from contemporary experts on the history of the Sioux tribes, including the Brules. But even an elliptical or obscure caption gives something of the viewpoint of the photographer or artist; the written words he gives to his picture are part of the visual document he creates.

A historian of the Sioux puts this "hostile" camp, as Grabill labeled it, on White Clay Creek, not "River Brule," and the date a few days after the surrender (on January 15, 1891) of fugitive Oglalas as well as Brules. Both had left their reservations at Pine Ridge and Rosebud, respectively, several weeks earlier. They had done so after new tensions—including the killing of Sitting Bull and the events at Wounded Knee within the month before the photograph was made—had been added to standing discontents from more than a decade of reservation life and recently reanimated by the new hopes held out by the Ghost Dance movement. Taking their tepees, they had left cabin life on the reservations to seek freedoms they once had known and to perform the new Ghost Dance.

Grabill caught the scene near the end of their abortive exodus—showing a village (or ville) of Brules and Oglalas, probably some 15 miles north of the Pine Ridge Agency. (The French, had translated as "Brulé" the Indian tribal name of Sicangu or Sichangxu ("burnt thighs"). The camp had been enlarged by some who did not leave their reservations until after the news of Wounded Knee (December 29, 1890). Around the time of the photograph there were an estimated 4,000 people, including 800 to 1,000 warriors, with 1,000 or more horses, 500 wagons, and about 250 travois. The scene stretched some three miles on both sides of White Clay Creek. Although placed in January, the scene shows only a few traces of snow, and a little ice on the creek, the snow and ice of the heavy blizzard that followed Wounded Knee having largely disappeared.

Wounded Knee, to the south and east of the area shown, was the dominating fact that led the occupants of the camp back to the reservations. But this was not all. For some time Major General Nelson A. Miles had been conducting a successful encircling operation—gradually reducing the off-reservation area of these tribes—a success formally recognized by the surrender. This event ended a historic month—from mid-December to mid-January 1890-91—as writers have recorded.

"Before Wounded Knee, despite more than ten years of reservation life . . . they still harbored illusions that the day of liberation would come . . . Indeed, this was the meaning behind the Ghost Dance movement that culminated in Wounded Knee." (Robert M. Utley, *The Last Days of the Sioux Nation,* 1963)

At Wounded Knee had come to an end "all the long and tragic years of Indian resistance on the Western plains." (Martin B. Schmitt and Dee Brown, *Fighting Indians of the West,* 1948). Mr. Brown is also the author of *Bury My Heart at Wounded Knee: An Indian History of the American West,* 1971.

This flow of history—both before and after this photograph—sweeps into the record a number of related individuals and events and including John J. Pershing, then a cavalry lieutenant under General Miles, assisting in the encirclement of these tribes, and shown in a Grabill group photo; and Colonel William F. Cody (Buffalo Bill) shown in a Grabill photo with Sioux Indians at Pine Ridge Agency, where he recruited some of the leaders, including Ghost Dance Brules, for his Wild West Show.

123

124

INDIAN CHILD AND PUPPY. Photograph by John C. H. Grabill. ©1891. LC-USZ62-17355

Grabill had printed on the mounts of many of his photographs of Indians and other Western life: "Official Photographer of the Black Hills & F.P. [Fort Pierre] R.R. and Home Stake Mining Co. Studios: Deadwood and Lead City, South Dakota."

Also: "A Handsome Reward given for detection of any one copying one of my Photographic Views."

125

A NEW ORLEANS MILK CART. Photograph by the Detroit Photographic Company. ©1903. LC-D4-16349

The company, known later as the Detroit Publishing Co., became one of the largest and most active general publishers of photographs in the country. Other examples of its work will be found in this section and in the sections on Architecture in the United States and on Transportation.

126

Chemistry Laboratory, Tuskegee Institute. Photograph by Frances Benjamin Johnston. 1903 or 1906.   LC-J694-161

The thoroughness with which Frances Benjamin Johnston's camera documented a variety of scenes of America, over a long period of years, is suggested in this view of students in a chemistry laboratory at Tuskegee Institute (then Tuskegee Normal and Industrial Institute). Already launched by the early 1890's on her professional career, which was to continue for more than half a century, she visited Tuskegee to record the growth in physical facilities in the two decades since its founding and the new construction (some by students) then under way, as well as curriculum-related views of students in classrooms, laboratories, outdoor study groups, and on field trips.

Her coverage of other educational institutions included Hampton Institute, Washington D. C. Public Schools, and the Art Students' League of Washington, and, among industrial subjects, coal mining in Pennsylvania and a shoe factory in Lynn, Mass. The breadth of the photographic record she left is indicated by other references in this book. (See "Introduction;" introduction to "Architecture in the United States;" and No. 160)

127

SAN FRANCISCO RUINS AFTER THE FIRE, APRIL
18TH AND 19TH, 1906. VIEW FROM FAIRMONT
HOTEL. Scene from panoramic photograph by
Johannes B. Moller. ©1906.   LC-USZ62-22066

Moller's series of eight photographs created
a panorama of the city's disaster. Panoramic
photography was popular in the late 19th and
early 20th centuries and Moller's subject, viewed
from the hilltop site of the Fairmont Hotel,
provided an unusual sweep of almost unrelieved
devastation.

128

SAN FRANCISCO EARTHQUAKE AND FIRE. Photograph by Arnold Genthe. 1906.

LC-USZ62-17359

129

SAN FRANCISCO EARTHQUAKE AND FIRE. Photograph by Arnold Genthe. 1906.

LC-USZ62-17358

A San Francisco photographer at the turn of the century, Genthe had come to the United States in 1895 from Germany, trained as a classical scholar. He was already achieving distinction for his photographic portraits and artistic studies and was "on location" when the earthquake and fire brought disaster to the city in 1906.

Many of his photographs reflect his concern with studies of individuals, as in the group in the foreground watching from the hillside the course of the fire in the city below and with studies of the shapes left by the earthquake, such as a row of houses set askew. He created what is generally considered the most outstanding photographic record of the disaster. The reproductions shown are from photographs in Genthe's own personal album. The original negatives are at the San Francisco Palace of the Legion of Honor.

130

WESTMINSTER STREET, PROVIDENCE, RHODE ISLAND. Photograph copyrighted by the Detroit Publishing Company. 1906.   LC-D4-19690

The concentration of the photographers who worked for the Detroit Publishing Co. on general city views, which included the daily activities of people, greatly enriches the records of the American urban scene in the early 20th century.

131

LITTLE ORPHAN ANNIE. Photograph by Lewis Wickes Hine. 1909. LC-USZ62-22016

A trained sociologist who used the camera to throw light on social conditions, Hine made photographs that were used extensively—particularly in the early years of the century—to illustrate surveys and reports. They have a continuing usefulness today to sociologists, writers, publishers, and others interested in the story he told. "Little Orphan Annie"—an "almshouse waif"— appeared in volume 5 (1914) of the six-volume *Pittsburgh Survey*, edited by Paul Underwood Kellogg of Survey Associates, Inc., and funded in large part and copyrighted by the Russell Sage Foundation.

In 1911 Hine was appointed staff photographer for the National Child Labor Committee to investigate child labor conditions in the United States. After visiting cities and towns in the Northeast and farmlands in the South, he returned with a series of photographs that were instrumental in the passing of a protective child labor law. Children at work in glass factories, mills, canneries, coal mines, at home in the tenements, and on the streets as messengers and paper boys are among the subjects of the approximately 5,000 photographs in this collection, some of which are accompanied by original glass-plate negatives.

132

THE SWEETEST STORY EVER TOLD. Pencil, pen-and-ink drawing by Charles Dana Gibson. 1910. Reproduced in *Collier's Weekly,* August 13, 1910. LC-USZ62-8637

Gibson was the creator of "The Gibson Girl," a popular feminine representation of the time, and also a political cartoonist for the old *Life* magazine.

133

BOYS PICKING SLATE IN A GREAT COAL BREAK-
ER, ANTHRACITE MINES, PENNSYLVANIA. One
half of a stereograph by Underwood & Underwood. ©1913.   LC USZ62-10107

Although the technology of the early 1900's
enabled photographers to record action instantaneously, many photographers posed their subjects in work or other action scenes. An examination of the original photograph clearly shows a
slight blur of one of the heads at the left of the
picture, an indication that in this picture the
boys had assumed fixed positions, and were not
actively engaged in the work indicated by the
title.

134

BLAST FURNACES, SOUTH CHICAGO. Lithograph by Joseph Pennell. 1916. [Although Louis A. Wuerth's *Catalogue of the Lithographs of Joseph Pennell,* 1931, locates the furnaces in Gary, Indiana, a handwritten note on the print itself places the scene in South Chicago.] LC-USZ62-22025

Between 1877 and 1922 Joseph Pennell produced 621 lithographs, many of them focusing on the industrial scene in the United States and Europe. In the introduction to the Wuerth book, Elizabeth Robins Pennell, the artist's wife, wrote: "In his own state of Pennsylvania, the coal breakers of Shenandoah and Wilkesbarre were for him transformed into 'Castles of Work.' Chicago, St. Louis, Gary were as inspiring in one way as French or English cathedral towns in another."

135

DEMPSEY THROUGH THE ROPES. Lithograph by
George Wesley Bellows. 1924. Printed by Bolton
Brown.   LC-USZ62-22026

Bellows caught the memorable moment on
September 14, 1923, at the Polo Grounds in New
York, when Jack Dempsey was knocked through
the ropes in the first round by Luis Firpo. Dempsey returned to the ring to win by a knockout in
the second round and retain his heavyweight
championship.

136

BILLIGE TOURISTENREISEN NACH NORD-AMERI-KA. Color poster by Bernd Steiner. 1928.

LC-USZ62-22056

Steiner used a part of the New York skyline to attract tourists for inexpensive trips to North America. One of the high buildings bears the name of the shipping and passenger line "North German Lloyd."

137

FARMER AND SONS WALKING IN THE FACE OF A DUST STORM, CIMARRON COUNTY, OKLAHOMA. Photograph by Arthur Rothstein for the Farm Security Administration. 1936.

LC-USF34-4052

The approximately 75,000 photographs (and their original negatives) in the Farm Security Administration-Office of War Information files were transferred to the Prints and Photographs Division in 1944. Notable for their quality as photographs, they provide a broad sociological and economic survey of the United States for the years 1935 to 1945. Agriculture, industry, American folkways, educational facilities, urban life, conservation of resources, and problems of sharecroppers are some of the subjects covered in this very important collection.

Besides Rothstein, three others in the remarkable group of photographers who produced the collection, under the directing intelligence of Roy E. Stryker, are shown next: Jack Delano, Marion Post Wolcott and Gordon Parks. Other photographers represented in the files include John Collier, Sheldon Dick, Walker Evans, Dorothea Lange, Russell Lee, Edwin Locke, Carl Mydans, Edwin Rosskam, Ben Shahn, and John Vachon.

Rothstein came to the FSA when it started, after completing his studies at Columbia University, and went on to a distinguished career in photojournalism, teaching, and writing. He became technical director of photography for *Look* magazine after the Second World War (when he was in Europe and the China-Burma-India areas) and served as director of photography for two years before *Look* ceased publication in 1971. In 1972 he presented to the Library of Congress his personal collection, which complements the work of his early career already in the FSA-OWI collection.

Dust storms and the "Dust Bowl" were a national concern in the 1930's, with John Steinbeck's novel *The Grapes of Wrath* adding literary documentation to that of the photographers sponsored by FSA.

138

139

POLISH TOBACCO FARMERS, WINDSOR LOCKS (VICINITY), CONNECTICUT. Photograph by Jack Delano for the Farm Security Administration. 1940.   LC-USF34-41573

Mr. and Mrs. Andrew Lyman were clients of the FSA. Another of his FSA assignments took Delano to Puerto Rico, where he documented the economic development effort directed by Rexford G. Tugwell (who had encouraged Stryker to undertake the initial FSA photodocumentation project). Delano became a permanent resident, and was named first director of the educational radio (and later television) station in San Juan. He had come to the FSA from art school in Philadelphia. Today, Delano and his wife write and illustrate children's books, returning to his initial interest in painting and drawing.

POST OFFICE DURING BLIZZARD, ASPEN, COLORADO. Photograph by Marion Post Wolcott for the Farm Security Administration. 1941.
                                        LC-USF34-59417

Although Mrs. Wolcott subsequently had less of a public career than some of the others of the FSA-OWI group, she had established herself not only as a photographer of unusual talent but also as one of those most heavily represented in the total product of the group.

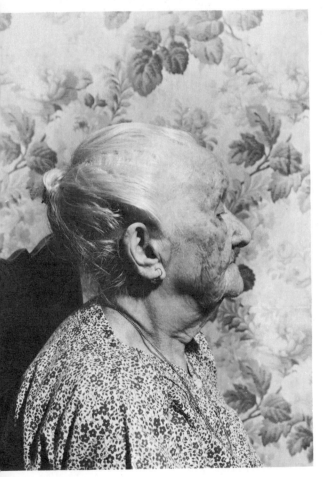

140

MRS. MARY MACHADO. Photograph by Gordon Parks for Office of War Information. 1943.

LC-USW3-31659-C

Gordon Parks was a member of the group of outstanding photographers who served in the photodocumentation programs conducted by the Office of War Information after their initiation by the U.S. Resettlement Administration and the Farm Security Administration.

This photograph was made under OWI auspices in Gloucester, Mass., in June 1943 and shows a 97-year-old grandmother of 11 men in the armed forces. The broad range of subjects covered by Parks in the FSA-OWI project included, besides other individual portraits, views of the fishing industry in Gloucester and of the Fulton Fish Market in New York; other seaside locations in New England and streets, Central Park, and other aspects of New York City; Washington housing and other views.

After surviving the disadvantages and difficulties that beset a young black in the depression period—working in the Civilian Conservation Corps and as a dining car waiter, piano player, basketball player, etc.—Parks' road to photography ran through the Southside Art Center in Chicago and a Julius Rosenwald fellowship, culminating in an invitation to join the Farm Security Adminis-

tration project, as it was then known, in 1942. As a dining car waiter he had seen a magazine with "a portfolio of photographs in it that I couldn't forget . . . across two pages was a memorable picture of a father and two sons running to their shanty in a dust storm [No. 137] . . . the photographers . . . all worked for the Farm Security Administration . . . I took it [the magazine] home and kept looking at those photographs and the names of the photographers for months . . ." On later getting the chance to go with FSA in Washington he wrote: ". . . Stryker had found me a place to stay temporarily. I would go ahead, find a house and send for my family later. At last I was on the move." (Gordon Parks, *A Choice of Weapons,* 1965)

Previously Parks had had a show at the Southside Art Center and Jack Delano, one of the FSA photographers [No. 138] whose work had inspired him, had attended. Another association was with Charles White [No. 201], the artist, who was working at the Center at the same time. White suggested that Parks apply with him for Julius Rosenwald fellowships; both did, and both won fellowships in the same year.

A prolific and committed creator, Parks has written prose, poetry, and music, directed motion pictures, and contributed photographs and texts for a number of articles in *Life* magazine.

Architecture in the United States

The Library's resources on American architecture comprise many collections, including the Historic American Buildings Survey (HABS) and the Pictorial Archives of Early American Architecture (PAEAA). Among the treasures in the Prints and Photographs Division is the collection of original architectural drawings of the late 18th and early 19th centuries, which includes drawings by William Thornton, Stephen Hallet, Charles Bulfinch, Benjamin Henry Latrobe, Alexander Jackson Davis, and Thomas U. Walter, all of whom worked on the public buildings of Washington, D.C., as well as on personal projects and designs.

Other unique collections include the work of Frances Benjamin Johnston, the first woman professional photographer, who was an influential figure early in the architectural preservation movement. The Library collections contain her photographs of the Deep South, systematically recorded in the 1920's and 1930's. Similarly, the work of Robert W. Tebbs, an architectural photographer of the 1930's and 1940's, is in the division's custody.

Supplemental documentation can also be found in the non-architectural files, particularly in the extensive collection of 18th- and 19th-century prints—engravings, wood engravings, lithographs of factories, churches, houses, schools, state capitols, etc.,—and in photographs beginning in the second half of the 19th century.

The Pictorial Archives of Early American Architecture was established in 1930 by Dr. Leicester B. Holland, Fellow of the American Institute of Architects and chief of the Division of Fine Arts, as the Prints and Photographs Division was then called. The purpose was to acquire by gift or bequest collections of photographic negatives, drawings, or other documents on American architecture from individual architects, photographers, and preservationists who no longer had an active use for them. With the aid of numerous grants from the

Carnegie Corporation of New York, some 10,000 negatives were acquired, printed, and cataloged for reference use.

The most important single collection on American architecture in the Prints and Photographs Division is the Historic American Buildings Survey. It originated in 1933 as a 10-week unemployment relief program for a thousand architects and architectural draftsmen, financed by the Civil Works Administration and administered by the National Park Service of the Department of the Interior.

The project of recording—in measured drawings, photographs, and data—our vanishing American architectural treasures was so valuable that it has been continued since 1934 on a permanent basis and in the last 15 years with great impetus. HABS has been a cooperative activity involving the National Park Service, which administers the program, the American Institute of Architects, which provides professional counsel, and the Library of Congress, which receives the completed records and makes them available for use.

The collection is continuously growing and now comprises more than 30,000 sheets of drawings, 40,000 photographs and 10,000 pages of architectural and historical data. All 50 states, the District of Columbia, Puerto Rico, and the Virgin Islands are represented. Many of the dwellings, churches, public buildings, shops, mills, and bridges which were a part of America's architectural heritage have disappeared (through fire, flood, decay, and urban renewal), and the best surviving records of them are to be found in the Survey.

Both HABS and PAEAA have shown how effectively government agencies and private organizations and individuals can work together in the interest of preserving for future study and other use important records of the history of architecture in the United States.

View of the East front of the Presidents House, with the addition of the North & South Porticos

B H Latrobe 1807

141

VIEW OF THE EAST FRONT OF THE PRESIDENT'S HOUSE, SHOWING THE ADDITION OF THE NORTH & SOUTH PORTICOS. Watercolor by Benjamin Henry Latrobe. 1807.   LC-USZ62-3068

The print is signed, at bottom right, "B.H. Latrobe 1807. S.P.B. [Surveyor of Public Buildings] U. States."

The south portico of the White House was completed in 1824, the north in 1829.

142

THE CAPITOL [ca. 1846] Daguerreotype attributed to John Plumbe, Jr.   LC-USZ62-46801

The earliest known photographic image of the Capitol was added to the division's collections in the summer of 1972, one of six daguerreotypes acquired by the Library. The photo shows the dome designed by Bulfinch after the War of 1812 and before the construction of the present, high cast iron dome.

Daguerreotypes have uniqueness because the technique does not permit the making of multiple prints. It is a direct positive technique, without use of a negative, with the image being created directly on a polished metal plate and viewed by reflecting light off the shiny silver surface. Norm-

ally, the image of a daguerreotype is reversed, owing to the absence of a negative/positive process (see also No. 72), but in this instance the photographer evidently used a reversing prism so the building appears to the viewer in its correct orientation.

The picture of the Capitol was reproduced by Plumbe, who came to be known as "the American Daguerre," in a lithographic print which he called a "Plumbeotype" and published around 1846. His Washington studio was part of a national chain of his galleries. Around 1847 his financial situation deteriorated, his Washington gallery was sold, and he moved to San Francisco. It was on the West Coast, early in 1972, that the discovery of the six daguerreotypes took place. It is hoped that

further research will establish more about Plumbe's career, including the uses he may have made of these daguerreotypes. The discovery itself is further evidence that historic and other rare additions to the files of prints and photographs can still take place, and provide new illumination of the past.

The other daguerreotypes show the White House before the office wings were built; the Patent Office—now the National Portrait Gallery—before the additions along 7th Street and 9th Street; two views of the General Post Office Building (now the Tariff Commission); and the Battle Monument on Charles Street in Baltimore.

DESIGNS

of a BUILDING

propofed to be erected at

RICHMOND in VIRGINIA,

to contain

A THEATRE, ASSEMBLY-ROOMS, AND AN HOTEL

by

B. HENRY LATROBE BONEVAL, Architect & Engineer.

Nunc est bibendum, nunc pede libero pulfanda tellus. Hor. Od. Lib.

Begun Dec.r 2.d 1797, finished Jan.y 8.th 1798.

143

DESIGNS OF A BUILDING PROPOSED TO BE ERECTED AT RICHMOND IN VIRGINIA, TO CONTAIN A THEATRE, ASSEMBLY, AND AN HOTEL. Watercolors by Benjamin Henry Latrobe Boneval. 1797 and 1798.

(1) Title page.   LC-USZ62-1220
(2) The auditorium as seen from the stage.   LC-USZ62-1221
(3) The ballroom.   LC-USZ62-1222

Although the designs were never executed, they show Latrobe's extensive knowledge of the theaters of England and the Continent. The designs, he noted on the title page, were "Begun Dec. 2d, 1797. finished Jan. 8th 1798." The need became real when the only theater in Richmond burned down. But the building proposed was beyond the range of public support at that time.

The title page is signed "By B. Henry Latrobe Boneval," the last an ancestral name he used to indicate his French derivation. The prop-room scene includes, as he wrote, "A groupe of theatrical apparatus, being almost a compleat inventory of the properties of the present Theatre at Richmond," to which he added a note "burnt in the night of the 23d of January 1798."

A VIEW OF THE MANSION OF THE LATE LORD
TIMOTHY DEXTER IN HIGH STREET, NEWBURY
PORT, 1810. Lithograph (hand-colored) by John
H. Bufford [184 - ?]

LC-USZ62-16402

Creator of "a splendid Fortune," Dexter was
styled a "Lord" by his friends. The caption states:
"The Statues or rather Images have no pretensions
to correctness of Character or even proportion but
are Faithfully delineated in order to convey a just
representation of one of the Whims of this most
truly eccentric Character whose many singularities
of Conduct and Speculations by which he acquired
from the smallest beginnings a splendid Fortune
are to be found in the Account of his Life Written
by Samuel L. Knap, Esq. & published at Newbury
Port . . ." (*A Life of Timothy Dexter Embracing
Sketches of the Eccentric Characters That Composed his Associates,* by Samuel L. Knapp, published in Boston in 1838, contains this view of the
mansion and figures but without the overprinting
of names.)

The figures principally represent military and
political leaders, including General Washington,
King George, William Pitt, Lord Nelson, "J. Jay,"
"N. Buonaparte," Louis XVI, "J. Adams," and "T.
Jefferson President;" also "Corn Planter," "Maternal Affection," "Travelling Preacher," and "Goddess Liberty"; and also "I am the greatest Philosopher in the Western World." Executed by a
local carver of ships' figureheads, the images have
been scattered in the course of time.

John P. Marquand, long a resident of Newburyport, wrote of Dexter in *Lord Timothy Dexter of Newburyport, Mass., First in the East, First
in the West, and the Greatest Philosopher in the
Western World* (1925), and in *Timothy Dexter
Revisited* (1960), one of his last published titles.

144

DESIGN FOR A CHURCH, WITH OVERLAY SHOWING AN ALTERNATIVE TREATMENT OF THE ENTRANCE AND TOWER. Pen-and-ink drawing with
wash by Charles Bulfinch [ca. 1821]

LC-USZ62-17350

Preliminary front elevations drawn for the
Unitarian Church which was built in 1821-22 at
6th and D Streets, N.E., Washington, D.C. In
1838 Bulfinch supervised repairs. After the Civil
War the church was altered by the addition of
buttresses and relocation of steps; it was later converted to use as a police court and was demolished
in 1900.

Bulfinch's scale, shown at the bottom right
of the drawing on the left, is "6 ft. to an Inch."

Viewing Dexter's complex character, Marquand wrote of him in the second book as "a peculiarly flamboyant eccentric," but also, as his epitaph said, as one who "gave liberal Donations for the support of the Gospel" and "for the benefit of the Poor And for other benevolent purposes."

The names of each Character are Inscribed on the Scotia of the Entablatures of the Column which being too small here to be made legible are placed perpendicular to their respective Statues

A View of the Mansion of the late LORD TIMOTHY DEXTER in High Street, Newbury port 1810

The Statues or rather Images have no pretentions to correctness of Character or even proportion but are faithfully delineated in order to convey a just representation of one of the Whims of this most truly eccentric Character whose many singularities of Conduct and Speculations by which he acquired from the smallest beginnings a splendid Fortune are to be found in the Account of his Life   Written by Samuel L Knapp Esq & Published at Newbury Port by John G Tilton

Published according to Act of Congress.

145

146

FRONT VIEW OF THE NEW YORK POST OFFICE
. . . MARTIN E. THOMPSON, ARCHITECT. Lithograph (hand-colored) by Endicott. 1845.
LC-USZ62-16945

The Middle Dutch Church on Nassau Street, built in 1727-31, was leased to the Government as a post office in 1844. Increasing commercial development of the neighborhood led to conversion of the building in spite of the fact of a prosperous congregation at this location. (I. N. Phelps Stokes, *Iconography of Manhattan Island,* vol. 3, 1918)

Postmaster Graham sent out a printed invitation, dated January 23, 1845, for the opening of the post office. According to Stokes, it was surmounted by a picture of the old church and lithographed by Endicott. The print shown here, which may be another view or an enlargement, bears the issue date February 1, 1845.

When the lease expired in 1860, the Government began to seek a new site. Since the Post Office Department was limited to $200,000 for this purpose, and the Nassau Street site was valued at $250,000, merchants, banks, and insurance companies, which did not want the Post Office to move, subscribed the $50,000 to make up the additional amount required. The Government then bought the property, which continued to be used as the Post Office until a new building was completed in 1875.

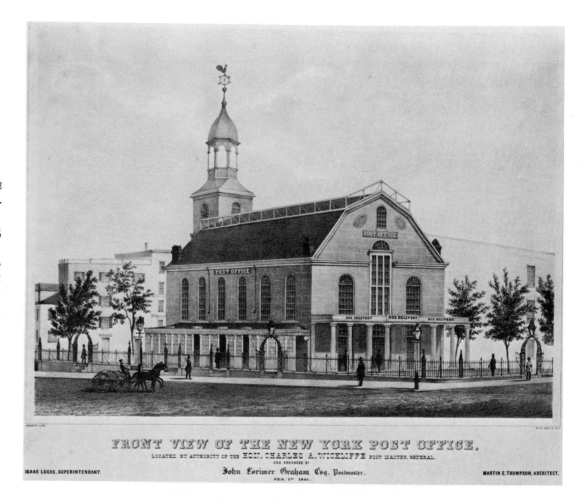

FRONT VIEW OF THE NEW YORK POST OFFICE,
LOCATED BY AUTHORITY OF THE HON. CHARLES A. WICKLIFFE POST MASTER GENERAL.
AND ARRANGED BY
John Lorimer Graham Esq. Postmaster.
FEB. 1ST 1845.

ISAAC LUCAS, SUPERINTENDANT.   MARTIN E. THOMPSON, ARCHITECT.

The print shows three signs for "Box Delivery". There were, in fact, 3,226 post office boxes in the building when it opened. "Such an imposing array of boxes shows at once the vast amount of business done in this office, especially when we take into consideration that there are nineteen mail letter carriers, who deliver their letters two or three times a day, besides twelve persons employed in the City Despatch letters." (*New York Evening Post,* January 17, 1845)

147

BIRD'S-EYE VIEW OF TRINITY CHURCH, NEW
YORK; RICHARD UPJOHN ESQ., ARCHT. Litho-
graph by John Forsyth and E. W. Mimee. ©1847.
LC-USZ62-425

The bird's-eye view was drawn by Upjohn,
the architect, to show the third and present
building, begun in 1841 and consecrated in 1846,
as it appeared in 1847. The view shows corner
buildings on Wall Street and Broadway, and
those to the west and north of the church, as
well as the shores of New Jersey. (I. N. Phelps
Stokes, *Iconography of Manhattan Island,* vol.
3, 1918) Upjohn was a leading American advo-
cate of the Gothic Revival mode.

148

IRANISTAN, AN ORIENTAL VILLE (NEAR BRIDGE-PORT, CONNECTICUT). Lithograph (hand-colored) by Sarony & Major. [Between 1847 and 1854]   LC-USZ62-16947

Iranistan was the home of the showman Phineas T. Barnum, who used for his model the pavilion erected by George IV at Brighton, England. It was a Saracenic villa (the print uses the French form of the word) designed by Leopold Eidlitz. Barnum invited a thousand guests to the housewarming. Among attractions aside from the architecture was an elephant which he kept there. When Jenny Lind required Barnum to deposit $187,000 in a London Bank as a guarantee of the contract for her American concert tour, which began in 1850, this condition forced him to mortgage Iranistan as well as other property. The villa burned down in 1858.

The print lists the height of the large dome as 90 feet and the length of the front as 124 feet.

149

MARY SHARP COLLEGE, AT WINCHESTER, TENN.
Painted by Chas. Guaita. Color lithograph by
Robertson, Seibert & Sherman [ca. 1860]

LC-USZ62-16952

Founded in 1850 as the Tennessee and Alabama Female Institute, the college faced early financial needs, which this print may have been intended to serve. Although it may be difficult to see in this reproduction, a man in the group of four in the lower right hand corner is showing the other three a copy of this lithograph, perhaps in the interest of fund raising.

The U.S. Bureau of Education reported that President Z. C. Graves, to whom the print is dedicated, "started with hardly any of the proper facilities, and it was three years or more before the college building was completed and occupied. After some time Mrs. Mary Sharp, a wealthy widow in the vicinity, made a gift to the Institute, and its name was changed to Mary Sharp College." President Graves, under whom it became the first women's college to require Greek and Latin for a degree, as reported by the U.S. Bureau of Education, served for 39 years. According to a report of the U.S. Commissioner of Education, the college was listed as having suspended operation in 1897-98.

150

NEW YORK CITY HALL. Photograph by William B. Holmes [ca. 1860]   LC-USZ62-22024

Completed in 1811 and still in service, New York City Hall has been called "undoubtedly the most important" new building erected in New York in the opening years of the last century, and "a monument to the taste and skill of its designers." (I. N. Phelps Stokes, *Iconography of Manhattan Island,* vol. 3, 1918)

The original design, accepted in 1802 and reflecting French Renaissance and American colonial influences, was the work of Joseph F. Mangin, a Frenchman, and his partner, John McComb. The following year, however, Mangin's role was abated when a curtailed plan was approved and McComb was appointed architect to superintend the construction. No mention of Mangin in connection with the building was made in the cornerstone ceremonies or on the inscribed foundation stone. McComb was "in sole charge of the design until its completion in 1812. . . . The French character of the New York City Hall is so exceptional [among McComb's architectural works] that it is probably to be accounted for by the connection of . . . Mangin with its original design." (*Dictionary of American Biography*)

151

RUINS OF THE PINCKNEY MANSION, CHARLESTON, S.C. Photograph by George N. Barnard [1865?]   LC-USZ62-10256

Sixty-one photographs appeared in 1866 in Barnard's famous album of *Photographic Views of Sherman's Campaign.* The prints were made from negatives taken in the field by Barnard, who was official photographer of the Military Division of the Mississippi.

Under this print, as under others in the album, is the line: "Photo from nature by G. N. Barnard." The fact that the photographer considered it necessary to include this information indicates the relative newness of direct-view photographs as illustrations in books in this country. The 1840's, 1850's, and 1860's saw a variety of techniques used for making illustrations and publishing them in books and weekly newspapers. They were not always accurately labeled in the publication. For example, a weekly newspaper might show woodcuts labeled as "Photographed by Brady" or as "From a Photograph by Brady," or as "Sketched by" an artist. The reproductions were in all cases made from photographs or sketches. Hence, readers by the 1860's were uncertain of what they were seeing. Barnard, therefore, made clear to viewers of his album that his illustrations were, in fact, "real-life photographs," whether as portraits of individuals or as scenes. To replace woodcuts, the principal form of book

illustration, by photographs in direct reproduction required new technology: the wet collodion process for wet-plate negatives. They made possible the production of multiple copies of prints that could be pasted directly into books as illustrations. The collodion technique was developed by Frederick Scott Archer of England in 1851.

152

MASONIC TEMPLE. Color lithograph by John J. Wynkoop [187 - ?]   LC-USZ62-16946

In Philadelphia the "new Masonic Temple, at Broad and Filbert Streets," was dedicated before a large gathering in 1873. It was designed by James H. Windrim as a display of historic architectural styles, with Oriental, Ionic, Norman, Egyptian, and other halls.

Lith. J. J. WYNKOOP, 164 S. 4th St., Phila.

MASONIC TEMPLE.

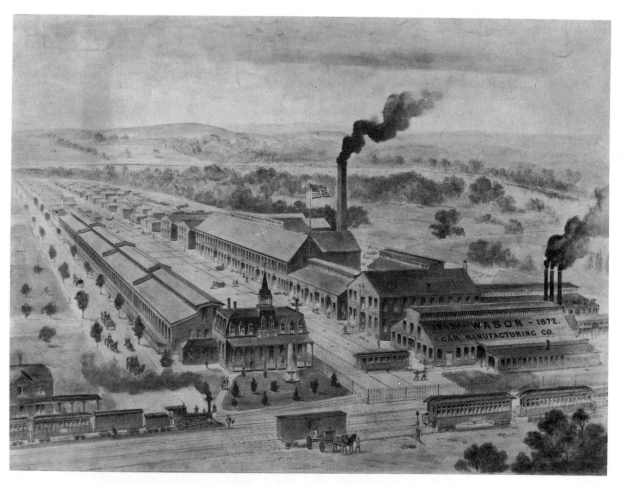

153

WASON MANUFACTURING COMPANY, SPRING-
FIELD, MASSACHUSETTS. Watercolor by Charles
R. Parsons & Lyman W. Atwater [1872?]
LC-USZ62-38239

This preliminary sketch for the following
Endicott & Company lithograph is an example of
the extensive collections of industrial and commercial architecture in the division.

154

WASON MANUFACTURING COMPANY OF
SPRINGFIELD, MASS. RAILWAY CAR BUILDERS,
CAR WHEELS AND GENERAL RAILWAY WORK.
WORKS AT BRIGHTWOOD, FIVE MINUTES FROM
SPRINGFIELD ON CONN. RIVER R. R. Sketched
and on stone by Parsons & Atwater. Color litho-
graph printed by Endicott & Company [1872?]
LC-USZ62-38240

The lithograph is a fairly exact copy of the
original drawing, with one notable exception:
the removal of the car from the conveyor to the
right of center. The empty conveyor indicates
more clearly that it was used to carry a completed
car to the railroad siding. A second change is
in the company name, on a middle foreground
building, from "Wason Car Manufacturing Co."
(as in lower right of print) to "Wason Manf'g
Co. Railway Car Builders." A boat has also been
added to the Connecticut River scene, appearing
near the smokestack.

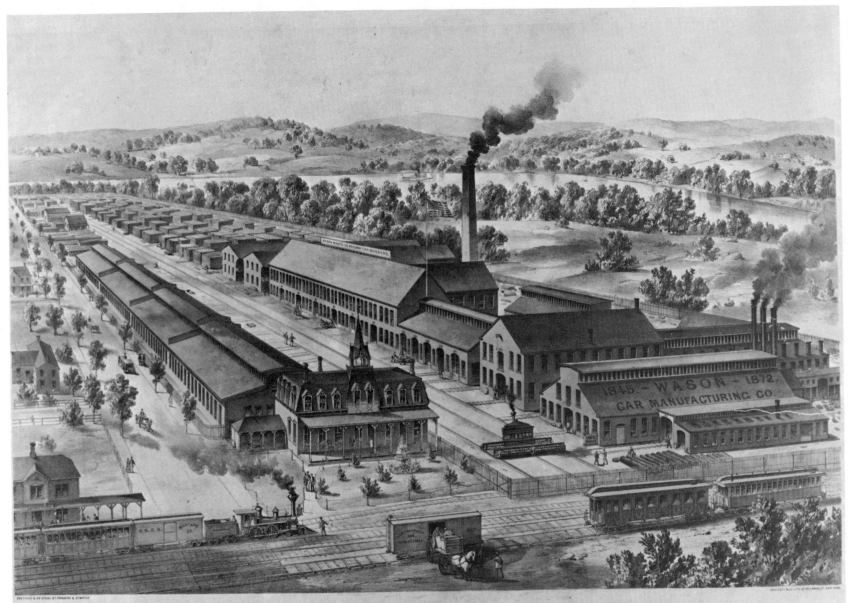

SKETCHED & ON STONE BY PARSONS & ATWATER.

ENDICOTT & CO. LITH. 27 BEEKMAN ST. NEW YORK.

WASON MANUFACTURING COMPANY of SPRINGFIELD, MASS.

RAILWAY CAR BUILDERS,

CAR WHEELS AND GENERAL RAILWAY WORK.

WORKS AT BRIGHTWOOD
Five minutes from Springfield
on Conn. River, R.R.

153

155

"The Breakers," Residence of Mrs. Cornelius Vanderbilt, Newport, R.I. Photograph copyrighted by the Detroit Photographic Company. 1904. LC-D4-16955

Among the scenes of American life recorded by the Detroit Photographic Co., also known as the Detroit Publishing Co., were private homes representing late 19th- and early 20th-century affluence.

The Breakers is now operated by the Preservation Society of Newport County.

156

AQUIA CHURCH, STAFFORD COUNTY, VIRGINIA.
Photograph by Francis Marion Wigmore.
PAEAA - VA., 90- —1-22

In the 1920's Francis Marion Wigmore photographed many of the old parish churches of Virginia, recording exteriors, interiors, churchyards, graveyards, memorial tablets, communion plates, etc. The photograph of Aquia Church, which is situated between Washington, D. C. and Fredericksburg, Va., is one of 253 negatives Wigmore gave in 1937 to the Pictorial Archives of Early American Architecture (PAEAA).

Aquia Church was rebuilt in 1757 after a fire had destroyed the building in 1751. "The interior preserves the square pews—though they are cut down—a gallery at the west end with a railing and columns which must be original, and an old three-decker pulpit which has all the earmarks of being the one that was always there. Aquia is a cruciform church and the pulpit is placed near the southeast re-entrant angle of the cross, the chancel occupying the eastern arm." (Henry Irving Brock, *Colonial Churches in Virginia,* 1930)

157

THE LINDENS, DANVERS, MASSACHUSETTS.
Photographed by Arthur C. Haskell, January 1934.
HABS, MASS. 5-Dav. 2-1

Built in 1754, by Robert ("King") Hooper, this house is among those most extensively covered in the Historic American Buildings Survey (HABS)—with 22 photographs and 29 measured drawings. When the building was photographed it was on Sylvan Street, in Danvers. It is, however, no longer in New England, having been taken down in 1934, removed, and reassembled in 1937 in Washington, D. C., by a private purchaser who still occupies it. Scenic French wallpaper was taken down before the house was moved and then restored at the new location. Piecemeal selling of various items in the house had begun before it was sold; the living-room woodwork was acquired for the William Rockhill Nelson Gallery in Kansas City, Mo., and other removals by purchase were in prospect at the time of the sale. The entire house was thoroughly documented by HABS just before its dismantling and was authentically restored and furnished after its reassembly in Washington.

158

THE LINDENS. PLAN OF GROUNDS. Pen-and-ink
measured drawing by Henry J. Murphy. 1934.
HABS, MASS. 5-Dav. 2,
Sheet no. 1 (Survey 2-33)

The garden was laid out about 1840.

159

THE LINDENS. MAIN ENTRANCE. Pen-and-ink
measured drawing by Adalbert B. Sziklas. 1934.
HABS, MASS. 5-Dav. 2,
Sheet no. 6 (Survey 2-33)

This drawing illustrates the extent of detail
available on "The Lindens" through the HABS
Collection.

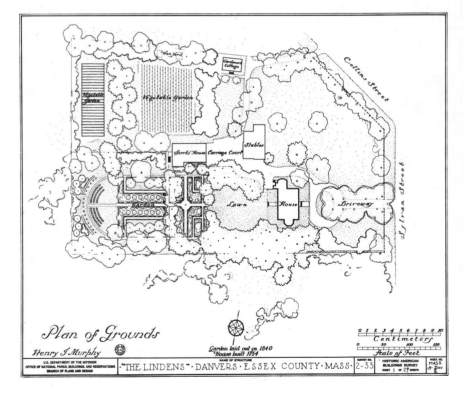

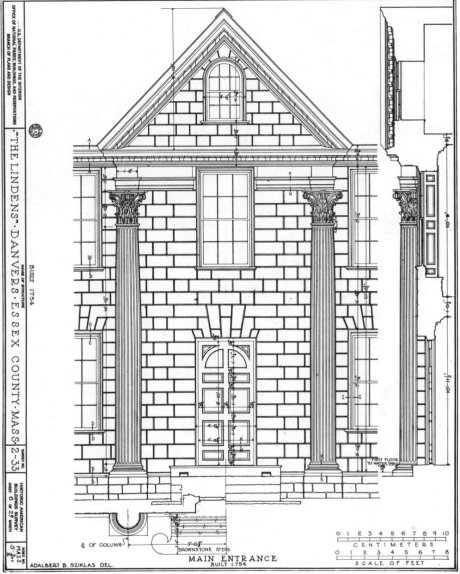

160

Cotton Press, Tarboro, Edgecombe County, North Carolina. Photograph by Frances Benjamin Johnston. 1936.   LC-J7–NC–2365

This early cotton press, which was removed to Tarboro from the nearby Norfleet Plantation, is "a lone survivor of a once numerous company." A colossal wooden screw filled a shaft in the center. Driven by mule power, the screw rammed loose cotton into wood forms to produce bales for shipping. A picturesque shed, which has not been preserved, covered the press, protecting the timbering as well as the cotton stored for baling from the weather. (Frances Benjamin Johnston, *The Early Architecture of North Carolina: A Pictorial Survey,* with *An Architectural History* by Thomas Tileston Waterman, 1941)

This photograph is from an extensive collection of systematic, documentary, photographic records of social and cultural aspects of Virginia and other Southern States which Miss Johnston's camera has preserved. Her interest covered other fields as well, leading, for example, to an extensive series of photographs of all phases of activity in the Washington public schools. The first American woman commercial photographer, she exhibited her work at the Third International Congress of Photography, held in Paris in 1900, where she was the only woman delegate.

161

LePrêtre Mansion, New Orleans, Louisiana. Pen-and-ink measured drawing by Alvyk Boyd Cruise. 1939.

HABS, LA. 36-Newor 18, Sheet no. 20 (Survey La-53)

As the Historic American Buildings Survey (HABS) notes, this tin Leader Head, which was painted pale blue, "may have been" on the Le-Prêtre Mansion, a residence on Dauphine Street which was built in 1836 by Frederic Roy for Joseph Coulon Gardette.

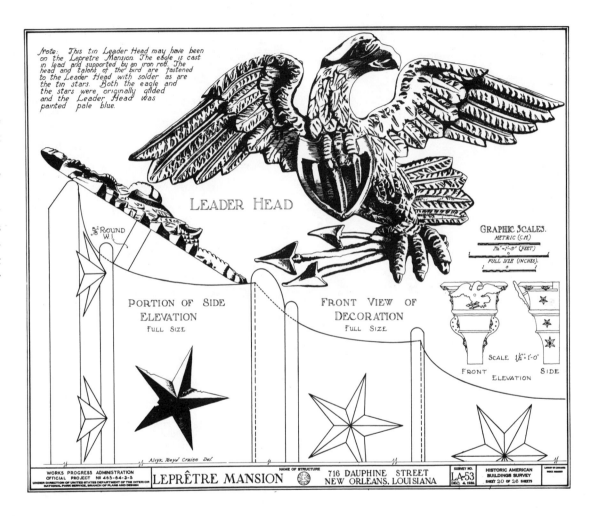

The Lively Arts

Pictorial records of the lively arts—the principal forms, old and new, of public entertainment—share in special degree the elusive character of ephemeral materials. Though the documents are often fugitive, the arts they record have long displayed a unique capacity to enlighten and enliven. Usually with little pretension to purpose other than to entertain, they make a strong claim upon us—largely on avocational time for most people—both for the experience of seeing and hearing and for that of participating in their creation as well. The collection and retention of items related to these popular arts is, therefore, essential if this significant part of man's past is to be understood.

Fortunately, a broad range of materials on this varied field is available in the division. Visual documents of the theater, tragic and comic, professional and amateur—and of other lively arts including music, dance, opera, the circus, television, sports, pictorial wit and humor, and the motion picture—appear in several collections. Thus, the celluloid Mickey Mouse shares space in the division with Arnold Genthe's portraits of the ballerina Anna Pavlova.

Although the greater portion of the material is American, a number of important groups of pictures relate to the theater in foreign countries, among them a collection of 52 nineteenth-century watercolors of French theatrical costumes, the prints of Jacques Callot and Wenceslaus Hollar, which provide additional material for costume study, and the collection of British cartoons with their satirical comments about the theater, chiefly of the late 18th and early 19th centuries.

The collection of approximately 2,500 stock posters from the 1870's through the early 1900's is virtually unique. Printed by such outstanding "paper" suppliers as the Strobridge Lithographing Company, Ferdinand Mayer & Company, W. J. Morgan & Company, and Gibson & Company, and ranging from one sheet to multiple sheets, they create an absorbing album of the American theater, including the minstrel show and the circus, during the late Victorian period.

The theater in America during the earlier part of the 19th century is documented by prints that came from the presses of the lithographers of the period — Currier & Ives, Thomas & Wylie, and Napoleon Sarony, among others.

Photographs provide unusual resources for the study of the theater, especially in the United States: original daguerreotypes of Jenny Lind and Junius Booth, original Mathew Brady Studio glass-plate negatives of theatrical personalities of the middle years of the 19th century, and the extensive collection of copyrighted photographs of the last quarter of the 19th century and the first decades of the 20th. The fullest photographic coverage of any actress or actor is the personal collection of Minnie Maddern Fiske, which numbers more than 2,000 prints.

The Prints and Photographs Division also has custody of the motion picture collection. While American films make up a majority of the titles, a large number of German, Italian, and Japanese films of the 1920's to 1940's have also been acquired by the Library. The collection contains more than 50,000 separate films, most of which were deposited at the Library for copyright. Over 8,000 of the titles have been added during the first four years (1968-72) of an agreement between the American Film Institute, a national center for progress in film art, and the Library of Congress.

Among various deposits or acquisitions of early films are more than 1,000 added through the purchase of the George Kleine Collection in 1947, and through such gifts as the Ernst Collection of early comedies and animated cartoons, the Allen Collection of documentary and entertainment films, the Mary Pickford Collection, and the Dunstan Collection of William S. Hart films. More recent acquisitions by gift or transfer include early films from the Edison Laboratory at West Orange, N.J., and the Theodore Roosevelt film collection from the Roosevelt birthplace in New York City. About one-tenth of the total items in the division's files is made up of silent films. Of more recent date are examples of educational and documentary television which were donated by both commercial and noncommercial producers, as well as film videotape recordings which were deposited for copyright.

A number of American artists have had a special interest in the entertainment scene, among them William J. Glackens, who is represented in both this section and in "United States History" for his work during the Spanish-American War; and Reginald Marsh, whose etchings of burlesque and vaudeville theaters of his time, evoke a part of a pattern of life for some in New York City, a pattern which had a special fascination for him and holds a special place in his work.

Mr BRAHAM in the character of ORLANDO.
to Mr THOs DIBDIN {the Author of the CABINET &c} this PRINT
is inscrib'd by his FRIEND......... ROBt DIGHTON.
Drawn, Etch'd,& Publ by Dighton, Chare Cross, march, 22, 1802.

162

MR. BRAHAM IN THE CHARACTER OF ORLANDO.
Etching (hand-colored) by Robert Dighton.
1802.   LC-USZ62-22037

Shown as Prince Orlando, in "The Cabinet,"
a comic opera for which he wrote much of the
music, John Braham received such plaudits in a
long career as "the first singer of the day," "the
greatest singer in Europe," and "an angel of a
singer" (Sir Walter Scott). Charles Lamb said
that in his quiet moments it was like "listening
to a cultivated gentleman talk intelligently to
you." Braham, a tenor, sang at age 13 at Covent
Garden.

163

J. WINANS IN THE CHARACTER OF "JOE" IN
THE NEW PLAY OF NEW YORK AS IT IS. Lithograph (hand-colored) by James Brown. Printed
and published by E. & J. Brown. ©1848.

LC-USZ62-15676

"New York as It Is" opened at the Chatham
with a familiar character Mose ("one of the
B'hoys") and Joe ("a Catharine Market Loafer"),
the latter part "inimitably played" by Winans
(George C. D. Odell, *Annals of the New York
Stage,* vol. 5, 1931). This genre had a vogue at
that time with "A Glance at New York" and
"Mysteries and Miseries of New York" also running in the same year and each having a role for
the character of Mose who, Odell observes, "must
have satisfied something in the broad human
sympathies of 1848!" While not as ubiquitous on
the New York stage, the character of "Joe" was
apparently in the same vein.

"YER DON'T THINK I'D STEAL APPLES DO YER!"

J. WINANS IN THE CHARACTER OF "JOE"

in the new Play of New York as it is. Playing at the Chatham Theatre New York.

Lith & Pub. by E. & J. Brown 140 Fulton St N.Y.

164

Jenny Lind. Daguerreotype by Mathew B. Brady [between 1850 and 1852]   LC-USZ62-8963

The daguerreotype was made during her triumphant American tour, 1850-52, which began at Castle Garden in New York City, under the sponsorship of the great showman Phineas T. Barnum. "The Swedish Nightingale" was engaged by Barnum to sing at $1,000 a night for 150 nights, with all expenses paid by the impresario. It was an unheard-of fee.

165

FIVE CELEBRATED CLOWNS ATTACHED TO SANDS, NATHAN CO.'S CIRCUS. Colored woodcut by Joseph Morse. Printed by Morse, M'Kenney & Co. ©1856.   LC-USZ62-14199

This immense poster, more than 11 feet in width, was printed in colored inks from huge woodblocks to advertise a traveling troupe of circus performers. Probably meant to be posted on the side of a barn, the poster was sent in advance of appearances, so that the time and place of the circus could be added locally. This is the earliest copyrighted pictorial poster in the Library of Congress, having been deposited (in a Federal District Court, as the law then required) in 1856.

American circus performers were popular at the time in England, so it is likely that this poster —or ones like it—attracted the French artist, Jules Chéret, when he was working in England. Inspired by the flat areas of color, lively outlines, and simple forms of the bold American posters, Chéret returned to France in the 1860's and initiated the style of poster design that culminated in the *Art Nouveau* movement and in the work of Toulouse-Lautrec, Pierre Bonnard, and Alfonse Mucha at the end of the 19th century.

166

MONS. BLONDIN'S WALK ACROSS THE CATARACT. Color lithograph by Charles Magnus & Company [1859]   LC-USZ62-22021

Jean François Gravelet Blondin of France, better known as Charles Blondin, crossed Niagara Falls several times in 1859 on a tight rope 1,300 feet long and 2 inches in diameter. He performed the feat in a variety of ways: blindfolded, pushing a wheelbarrow, carrying another man.

Blondin's celebrated exploits, pictured and reported, reached deeply into the public mind. Special trains and grandstands evidenced the public interest in his performances. Responding to "an excited delegation of clergymen, troubled about the conduct of the war," Lincoln said to them: "Gentlemen, suppose all the property you were worth was in gold, and you had put it in the hands of Blondin to carry across the Niagara River on a rope, would you shake the cable, or keep shouting out to him, 'Blondin stand up a little straighter!—Blondin, stoop a little more— go a little faster—lean a little more to the north —lean a little more to the south'? . . . (Carl Sandburg, *Abraham Lincoln: The War Years,* vol. 2, 1939)

The famous "Maid of the Mist" is shown below the figure of Blondin.

MONS. BLONDIN'S WALK ACROSS THE CATARACT.

167

EDWIN BOOTH AS HAMLET. Chromolithograph by Bencke & Scott. ©1873. LC-USZ62-15683

One of the division's most frequent requests today is for information about an "oil painting in my collection, which was entered according to Act of Congress in the office of the Librarian of Congress." The copyright statement, itself, however, is an indication that the work in question is a chromolithograph and not an original oil painting. During the 1870's and 1880's, photo-mechanical color reproductions of paintings, like the ones which can be purchased today, were not being published; the various printing methods by which these reproductions are now made were still to be developed. Nevertheless, pictures for home decoration produced by other printing processes were offered to the public. One of these was chromolithography, a process intended to produce a print to resemble an oil painting. This process attained a popularity that was to last until the development of the more sophisticated methods of color reproduction. To gain his desired results, the chromolithographer used oil paints, treated the paper so that the surface would resemble brush strokes, and often backed the print with canvas or canvas-like cloth on which the phrase "warranted oil colors" was occasionally stamped.

168

CALLIOPE! THE WONDERFUL OPERONICON OR STEAM CAR OF THE MUSES. Color lithograph by Gibson & Company. ©1874. LC-USZ62-1027

Named for Calliope, the Muse of epic poetry, this instrument of steam and air whistles was activated by a keyboard. It was used on river-boats and in carnivals and circuses, often being a feature of "the circus parade."

CALLIOPE! THE WONDERFUL OPERONICON OR STEAM CAR OF THE MUSES.
AS IT APPEARS IN THE GORGEOUS STREET PAGENT OF THE GREAT

EUROPEAN ZOOLOGICAL ASSOCIATION!

BRITISH MUSEUM. ROYAL COLISEUM. GALLERY OF ART. WORLD'S CONGRESS AND GIGANTIC CIRCUS! 12 Tents! 900 Men and Horses! One Ticket Admits to All!

169

THEATRICAL WIGS, BEARDS, &C. Photolithograph by the Graphic Company [187–]

LC-USZ62-15682

Advertisements like this one for a supplier of theatrical hairpieces are sources of exact knowledge of designs for the theater at particular periods of its history. This item also suggests some of the diversity of hair styles advertised for stage use a century ago.

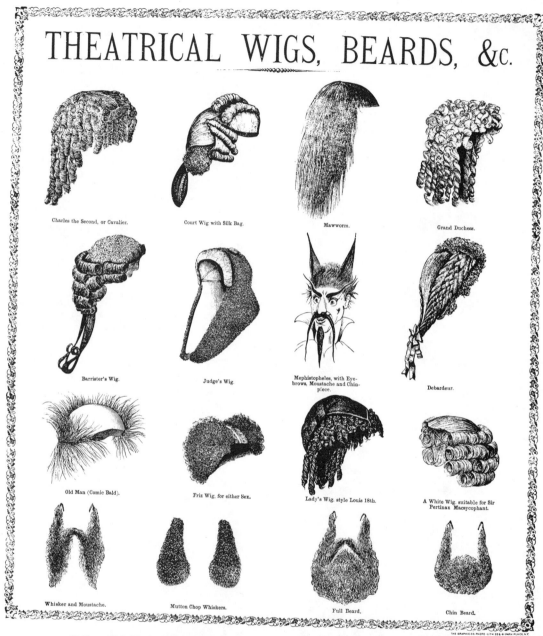

170

170

LEWIS MORRISON'S MAGNIFICENT NEW FAUST. THE BROCKEN SCENE. Color lithograph by the Springer Litho. Company. ©1889. LC-USZ6-453

When Morrison introduced his version of *Faust* at the Grand Opera House, Brooklyn, on April 1, 1889, with "a capable company," the *New York Herald* also reported that the "weather interfered with the electrical effects, but the spectacular features were well received." These features included "The Brocken Scene" depicting the legendary Walpurgis Night on The Brocken, highest peak in the Harz Mountains of Germany. At his death in 1906 *The New York Times* (August 20) reported that Morrison, who had appeared with Tommaso Salvini, Edwin Forrest, Edwin Booth, and Charlotte Cushman, "of late years . . . has been best known for his characterization of Mephistopheles in *Faust*."

Like many of the other theatrical posters in this book, no place of performance is printed on this advertisement; such "stock posters" could be used wherever the company played, with the local time and place added on a pasted label.

171

OLE OLSON. "LET ME SEE YOUR TONGUE."
Color poster designed by A. M. Willard. Printed
by Shober & Carqueville. ©1890.
LC-USZ62-15354

Archibald M. Willard is best known as the
artist of the "Spirit of '76."

Swedish dialect was a part of Olson's performances, on New York and other stages, in the
1890's. Commenting on his appearance at the
Third Avenue Theatre in New York, George C.
D. Odell wrote: "Ole Olson transported us to
far-off scenes, at least with his dialect." (*Annals
of the New York Stage*, vol. 5, 1931)

172

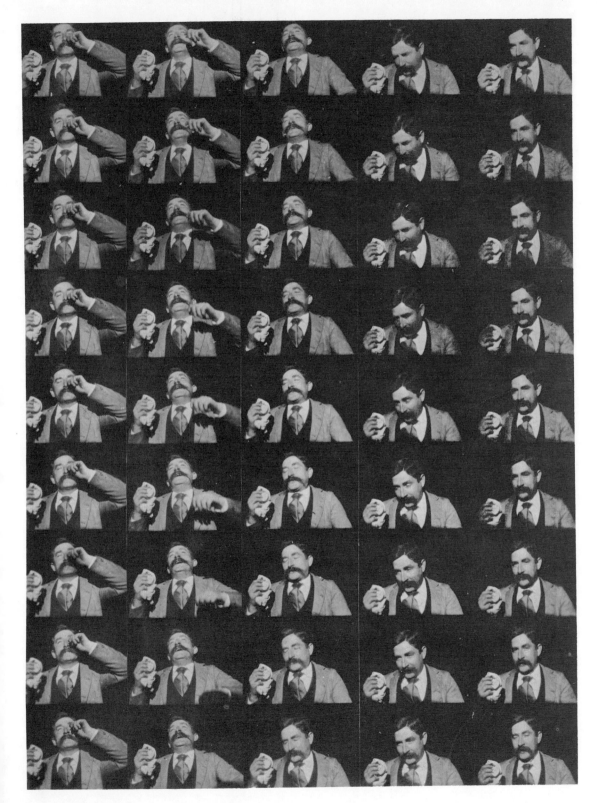

EDISON KINETOSCOPIC RECORD OF A SNEEZE.
Photograph by W. K. L. Dickson. ©January 7,
1894.   LC-USZ62-536

The earliest identifiable material submitted
for the copyright of a moving picture, in the
Prints and Photographs Division's files, is this
Kinetoscopic record of Fred Ott, a Thomas A.
Edison employee, and his sneeze. Earlier materials were submitted for the same purpose but
the applications were not fully completed, or, in
one case, the identity of the submission remains
unknown. This sequence had to be registered in
still-print form because the copyright law did
not provide for motion pictures until 1912.
Dickson was the project supervisor for Edison
in development of the Kinetoscope process, and
a skilled photographer who made some of the
most familiar pictures of Edison himself. "The
Sneeze" was filmed at the Edison laboratory/
studio in West Orange, N.J.

173

SANDOW. Photograph by B. J. Falk. ©1895.
LC-USZ62-22030

Eugene Sandow, "The Strong Man of Europe" and "The Great Sandow," an early leader in promoting physical exercise and development, was widely publicized by Florenz Ziegfeld as well as by his own extensive appearances and writings. His muscular poses made him one of the more familiar figures of his time, and, in a sense, a folk character. His name became a virtual synonym for physical strength and a symbol of the power of will in achieving such prowess.

SANDOW.

174

ANNA HELD. Photograph by Aimé Dupont.
©1900. LC-USZ62-22031

Miss Held is shown in the fashion of the time, as recorded by a Fifth Avenue photographer. After hearing Anna Held as a *chanteuse* in Paris in 1890, singing "Won't you Come and Play Wiz Me?," as a show business legend has it, Florenz Ziegfeld determined she could reach greater fame on the New York stage under his tutelage than in Paris and, somewhat later, that she should become Mrs. Ziegfeld. Both events came about, and Anna Held came to symbolize aspects of an American era including the fashionable hourglass figure, which was both emulated and envied, and "milk bath" publicity. She was featured in theatrical roles, some of which were later seen to be forerunners of the Ziegfeld Follies. On July 9, 1907, the first edition of the Follies opened in New York with a chorus consisting of "Fifty Anna Held Girls."

PRIMROSE & DOCKSTADER'S GREAT AMERICAN MINSTRELS. BACK AGAIN, LEW DOCKSTADER, THE MAN WHO MAKES MILLIONS LAUGH. Lithograph by H. C. Miner Lithograph Company. ©1898   LC-USZ6-490

". . . He made more Americans laugh than any other man of his time. His going brought to a close a definite period of our national humor. The old school of minstrelsy died with its greatest minstrel." (James C. Young, *The New York Times,* November 2, 1924) With George Primrose, Dockstader had formed "the most famous minstrel combination that the art ever knew."

While minstrelsy survived into this century as a popular entertainment form, Dockstader was considered the last great star of its major era and Primrose and Dockstader the last minstrels to tour the large cities. In this lithograph Dockstader appears in the apparel that had become a trademark for audiences all over America—trick shoes, oversized trousers and coat, and tall hat. Dockstader's success also turned in part on his fondness for political monologue, giving spice to his sketches, and on imitation and caricature of famous persons, including President Theodore Roosevelt, in gestures, stride, and speech. Always working to keep his material up to date, he continually sought topical and personality themes and situations, national or local, as occasion suggested.

"His death, as truly as Garrick's, diminished the public stock of harmless pleasure." (*Dictionary of American Biography*)

THE HUMAN LIZARD AND THE HUMAN FROG.
Pen-and-ink drawing by William J. Glackens in
Scribner's Magazine. October 1899.

LC-USZ62-17415

Out of the days of vaudeville, this is one of
five drawings in the Library's collection from a
series of 18 illustrations by Glackens for an article
on "The Vaudeville Theatre," by Edwin Milton
Royle.

Reporting on backstage news and inter-
views, Royle wrote of the acrobatic vaudeville
performers Glackens shows sharing a dressing
room with another performer standing at the
table. The two were "middle-aged, bald-headed,
bandy-legged little men" who, after changing,
became "a green-striped bundle of assorted legs
and arms"—the Human Lizard, and his "partner
in the Batrachian business," the Human Frog.
Both were "loosenin'up," one explaining "yer
legs git stiff, ye know" with time.

"And the striped bundle folded in and out
on itself and tied itself in bows, ascots, and four-
in-hands until every joint in the actor's body was
cracking in sympathy.

"Meanwhile his partner was standing apart
with one foot touching the low ceiling, and his
hands clutching two of the clothes-hooks. . . ."

On the callboy's signal to go on they "un-
wound and, getting their heads and tails under
their arms, glided away for the stage."

"The Vaudeville Theatre," Royle wrote, "is
an American invention. There is nothing like it
anywhere else in the world. . . . [it] is now doing
business with us under the patronage of the royal
American family. . . . Fourteen years ago this may
have been a dream in a Yankee's brain; now it is a
part of us. The strictly professional world has been

looking for the balloon to come down, for the fad
to die out, for the impossible thing to stop, but
year by year these theatres increase and multiply,
till now they flourish the country over."

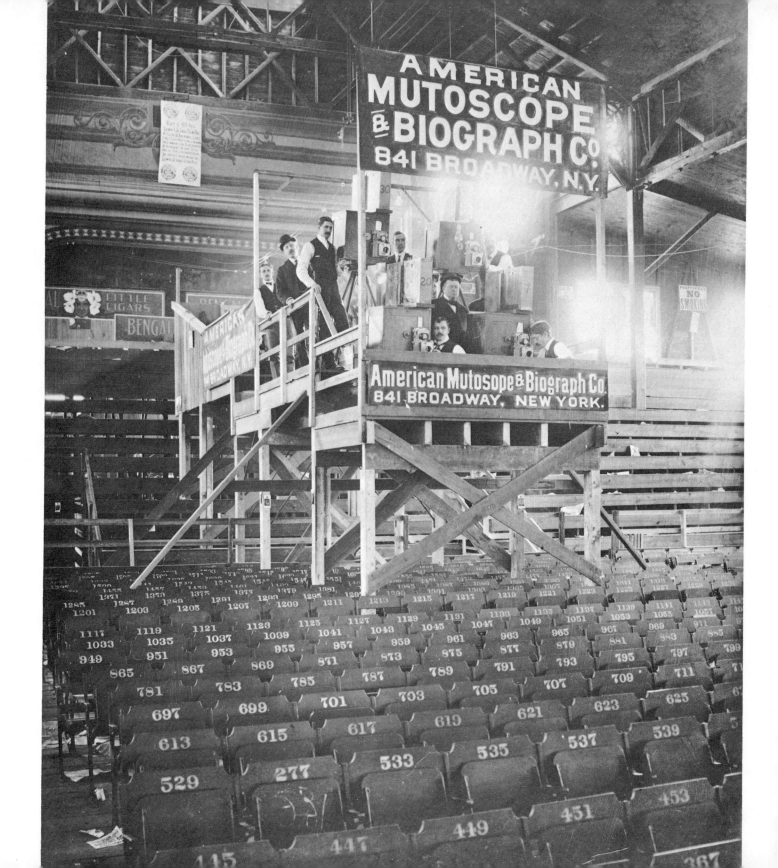

INTERIOR OF THE CONEY ISLAND (NEW YORK) CLUB HOUSE. Photograph by the American Mutoscope & Biograph Company. ©1899.

LC-USZ62-8207

The American Mutoscope & Biograph Company's cameras are shown in readiness to photograph a prizefight. Such fights provided the footage for some of the first movies that lasted longer than the early short features, which often ran only 50 feet or less.

Late in 1899, for example, the American Mutoscope & Biograph Co., a major early producer of films of events and special subjects, "shot" motion pictures of the James J. Jeffries-Tom Sharkey fight of 25 rounds at Coney Island. While the company was also organized to produce still positives that could be mounted on flip-cards for fast sequential individual viewing on a Mutoscope (which gave the illusion of movement), it soon found the greater opportunity lay in producing film for projection for an audience. Aided by the high public interest in prizefighting, the infant motion picture industry could reach out to this ready market for feature-length or longer film. Since it was limited in the number of scenes it could show, the Mutoscope was more adaptable to penny arcades and peep shows. Nonetheless, the device, providing newsreel as well as entertainment subjects, spread to many parts of the country, and may still be seen at some seaside or other resorts.

While still in an early stage, the technology of film was already at hand for prizefight demonstration and for continuing development. W. K. L. Dickson, a photographic specialist of marked accomplishment who had been project supervisor for Thomas A. Edison in creation of the Kinetoscope, was closely associated, with others, in the development of the Biograph, as well as the Mutoscope, processes.

The American Mutoscope & Biograph Company's preparations for coverage of the Jeffries-Sharkey fight foretold the rapid ascendancy of film. William A. Brady, later the Broadway theatrical producer, was the fight impresario. He had made the "daring proposal" to the American Mutoscope and Biograph Co. of a motion picture of the fight, to be held indoors at the Coney Island Athletic Club. All previous efforts at making such motion pictures under lights had failed, however, for lack of sufficient illumination. But the company took the unprecedented step of massing 400 arc lights over a ring slightly reduced in size.

Using some seven miles of negative, the company was able to offer more than a mile (5,575 feet) of usable film to the trade. "The ceiling of throbbing electric arcs broiled the fighters in the ring . . . . Between rounds the seconds held umbrellas over the corners while attendants fanned and ministered to the fighters.

"The electrical connections overhead, loaded to the limit with current, grew so hot that they threatened to burn out. Biograph workmen raided the refrigerator of an adjacent saloon and applied ice to the sizzling plugging boxes and switches . . . ." (Terry Ramsaye, *A Million and One Nights,* 1926)

Nonetheless, the demonstration showed that existing technology could produce such films and with indoor lighting. A sidelight reported by Ramsaye indicates the pioneering and, in the eyes of the promoters, the "piratical" nature of the small industry at that time. An employee of another early motion picture company organized a plot to divide camera apparatus among several co-conspirators, conceal the items under their coats, carry them into the arena in the press of the crowd, and shoot unauthorized pictures from their seats. Although this firm booked a print to a firm of vaudeville producers at $200 a week for a time, according to Ramsaye, Biograph, through an injunction Brady obtained, finally won the field for its authorized film. The prizefight led to progress in motion pictures in several respects, e.g., after only a quarter century "four or five motion picture arcs would serve as well as the four hundred Biograph used over the ring that night."

The division has 62 feet of 16 mm film of

180

178

BUFFALO BILL'S WILD WEST AND CONGRESS OF ROUGH RIDERS OF THE WORLD. A CONGRESS OF AMERICAN INDIANS. Color lithograph by Courier Litho. Company. ©1899.   LC-USZ62-1164

This lithograph was produced in Buffalo—an indication that color printmaking techniques were not limited to New York, Philadelphia, and other Eastern Seaboard cities. Colonel Cody organized his spectacular show in 1883, and took it on tour in Europe as well as in the United States. He is credited with giving an early impetus to the "Western Hero" business, which has come to embrace novels, motion pictures, radio, television, music, and rodeos.

179

WILLIAM F. ("BUFFALO BILL") CODY DURING HIS RUN IN OLYMPIA STADIUM, LONDON. Photograph [1903]   LC-USZ62-22029

An album of 36 photoprints of Buffalo Bill and his troupe at the Olympia Stadium was presented to the Library of Congress in 1925 by Maj. Sherman Miles. Earlier, in 1887, performances at Queen Victoria's Jubilee had made Cody and his troupe an international success. In this country their appearance at the Chicago World's Fair of 1893 was a memorable event for many Americans.

180

MRS. FISKE, MARY OF MAGDALA. Color poster designed by Ernest Haskell. Printed by the Grignard Litho. Company. ©1903. LC-USZ62-17357

One of the leading ladies of the American stage, Minnie Maddern Fiske, with (Frederick) Tyrone Power (1869-1931) as Judas, presented in 1902 Paul Heyse's biblical drama, which ran for more than 100 performances. Mrs. Fiske's own collection of photographs, made during her long career and numbering more than 2,000, is one of the special resources of the division in the lively arts field.

Ernest Haskell was a well-known designer of posters, and his designs were sought by collectors during the poster craze of the 1890's. The design of this poster is closely related to the stylized work of the French, Austrian, and Czech poster artists of the *Art Nouveau*. The mosaic and the Pompeiian furniture were conscious attempts to suggest antiquity in a modern style.

MRS. FISKE.
Mary of Magdala.

181

ANNA PAVLOVA. Photograph by Arnold Genthe
[after 1911]   LC-G389-1163

In addition to the photographs Genthe made of the San Francisco earthquake and fire, Chinatown in San Francisco, the Yosemite Valley, Charleston, S.C., New Orleans, and other cities, and of Japan, Korea, Guatemala, and Cuba, he also was professionally engaged in making portraits and artistic studies of his own immediate circle of artists, musicians, writers, society women, public figures, and dancers, including Isadora Duncan and the Duncan dancers, The Library's collection of approximately 10,000 glass-plate negatives and prints represents virtually his entire life work. Among them are several photographs of Pavlova.

Genthe met Pavlova in San Francisco when she was performing there with Mikhail Mordkin, her dancing partner. The Barbary Coast had been rebuilt after the earthquake and fire and new dances were in full swing—the Turkey Trot, the Texas Tommy and the Grizzly Bear. Genthe wrote that he arranged a party for Pavlova and Mordkin to see the waterfront nightlife, the arrangements including a detective, at the police chief's suggestion, to go along "in case of emergency."

The party visited one of the famed dance halls which he described as "a vast 'palace' of gilt and tinsel with a great circular space in the center and around it a raised platform with booths for the spectators. We took our place in one of these. Below us on the floor, to the barbarous sound of tom-tom, cymbal, horn and banjo, a medley of degenerate humanity whirled around in weird dance steps . . . ."

After a time of watching, Pavlova and Mordkin stepped down to the floor, where Mordkin had to pay the customary ten-cent fee. . . . Nobody knew who they were, and nobody noticed them as they began to feel out the barbaric rhythm with hesitant feet. Gradually they were carried away by it and, oblivious to their sordid surroundings, they evolved, then and there, a dance of alluring beauty.

"Gradually, one couple after another stepped aside to watch, forming an astonished circle at the edge of the floor. When Pavlova and Mordkin had finished, there was a moment of silence, followed by wild bursts of applause. The men stamped and threw their caps into the air and the women clapped, calling out 'More! More!' They made no attempt to crowd in around Pavlova or to speak to her, and when she passed through the circle to get to the booth, a respectful lane was made for her."

Genthe concluded his account: "This incident has always seemed to me a thrilling example of the power of great art. Pavlova was touched to tears by it, and she said, years afterward, that the tribute of the sorry rabble that night had meant more to her than decorations she had received from the crowned heads of Europe." (Arnold Genthe, *As I Remember,* 1936)

SELIG PRESENTS THE MOVING PICTURE COWBOY. A WESTERN COMEDY IN TWO REELS. SELIG PRESENTS. UNION PACIFIC. TOM MIX DOING STUNTS. THE WAY HE TOLD THE STORY, AND WHAT HE REALLY DID. A WESTERN COMEDY IN TWO REELS.

182

SELIG PRESENTS THE MOVING PICTURE COWBOY. A WESTERN COMEDY IN TWO REELS. Color lithograph by Goes Litho. Company. ©1914.
LC-USZ62-19684

This poster was made in Chicago at the height of Tom Mix's early career as a Western star when he was appearing for the Selig Company (Selig Polyscope Co.) of Chicago, one of the major pioneers in the early films. Mix had come from Mix Run, Pa. He later settled in Oklahoma —where he bought a ranch and exercised his high skills as a horseman. Selig was looking for a good ranch location and someone who knew the territory. The film company made a picture on the ranch, and Mix began to work for Selig, first as a general adviser and specialty man, then filling acting parts. Between 1911 and 1917 he made between 70 and 100 one- and two-reelers, with predominantly Western backgrounds, for Selig. In many he was featured as star, author, and director, and other posters in the Division's collection give him such added listings. Mix joined Fox in 1917 and began a further career as a molder of the modern Western.

One of the most successful of all actors at the box office, he had appeared by 1929 in many more pictures than any other motion picture star. His style had largely supplanted that of an earlier Western star, William S. Hart, who is represented in the division by the Dunstan Collection of his films. Mix was one of the first to exploit the high, large-brimmed hat, usually white, and other new "Western" apparel. His influence was away from the realism of earlier models and toward a greater emphasis on showmanship. This has been variously defined by writers on the motion picture as relating to "a never-never land," "a male dream world, which Hollywood sold to the world as the American West," a world of "simple, superficial, shoot-it-out plots," and as "an abstraction, a convenient, stylized backdrop against which to act out . . . simple dreams of heroism."

183

NAZIMOVA IN OSCAR WILDE'S "SALOME." Color poster. 1922.   LC-USZ62-22019

This motion picture poster reflects the decor of the film itself. Sets and costumes were by Natacha Rambova, based on the book illustrations Aubrey Beardsley published in 1894. Nazimova was Mrs. Charles Bryant.

IRVING PLACE BURLESK. Etching by Reginald Marsh. 1929. LC-USZ62-22033

Starting soon after 1900, a group of artists in New York City used real-life, unromanticized scenes of urban America as the subjects of their prints, drawings, and paintings. William Glackens (whose work is shown elsewhere in this book), John Sloan, and Robert Henri were among the first of these "Ashcan School" artists, as they were dubbed by critics, and Reginald Marsh took the same direction in his work somewhat later.

Marsh was a painter and socially conscious political cartoonist, as well as a prolific print-maker. Like many of his colleagues, he had an attic studio north of Greenwich Village, near 14th Street, at a time when the area, before its more recent development through department stores and other firms, was declining.

The Irving Place Theatre, in the same area, saw its own cycle of distinction and decline. Irving Hall, a site for dramatic, musical, social and other events, had occupied the southwest corner of Irving Place and 15th Street from its opening in 1860 to 1888, when it was demolished to make way for the Amberg German Theatre, opened late the same year. Known from the early 1890's as the Irving Place Theatre, it nonetheless maintained strong German associations until 1917, when, because of the atmosphere of World War I, its regular performances in the German language came to an end. In 1918, under the aegis of Maurice Schwartz, it ushered in the professional Yiddish art theatre movement. In 1929, the year of Marsh's etching, the *New York Times* (December 22) described it as "the famous old Irving Place Theatre, where German singers had trod the boards and which now plays burlesque to crowded houses. . ."

It had become, like the Hudson Burlesk in Union City, N.J., an aspect of the broad metro-politan milieu of Union Square, Coney Island, the Bowery, people in subway and street views, and other aspects of the urban *human* scene Marsh sought to depict. For the Whitney Museum of American Art's catalogue and traveling exhibi-tion, Lloyd Goodrich wrote: ". . . wherever the crowds were thickest and the human animal dis-played his infinite variety, he found his subjects. One of his dominant themes was the public pur-suit of pleasure in its myriad forms—theatres, burlesque houses, night clubs, dime-a-dance joints, Harlem dance halls. Early in his career he fell in love with Coney Island and became the first painter to fully exploit its flamboyant wonders . . . . Burlesque had no more devoted student. . . ." (In *Reginald Marsh,* 1955)

© Walt Disney Productions

185

MICKEY MOUSE. Painting on cellulose acetate from the studio of Walt Disney [194 – ?]

LC-USZ62-22017*

Animation of motion pictures involves photographing a series of still images, each slightly different from the other, which will give the effect of movement when projected at the rate of about 24 frames per second. Thus, more than 14,000 separate exposures are needed to make a 10-minute animated film. The Walt Disney Studios used a system of painting each figure in a cartoon and the elements of the background or scene on separate sheets of transparent celluloid that were superimposed in the animation camera. Only the character or object that moved in a given scene required a new painting, so the amount of elaborate redrawing could be kept to a minimum. This picture of Mickey Mouse is one of those paintings on celluloid, which is the reason he is not shown in a setting.

Artists' Prints

In all periods, prints by artists have had in common an inner life more subtle and often more complex than prints made merely to illustrate, record, or propagandize. Reproduced in this section are some of the masterpieces of graphic art in the Prints and Photographs Division: a group of brilliant impressions, without limitation of the period or nationality of their creators, to indicate both areas in which the collections are strong and directions that acquisitions are currently taking.

During the Library's first century the growth of its picture collections proceeded on a haphazard basis, without specific plan or professional guidance. Soon after the occupation of the new building in 1897, however, the widow of Gardiner Greene Hubbard, in presenting her husband's collection to the Library, stipulated that the Librarian appoint a superintendent of an art gallery to be designed to house the excellent works of Dürer, Mantegna, Rembrandt, and other master printmakers in the Hubbard Collection. In addition, upon her death in 1909 she provided a fund to yield an annual income for the purchase of prints.

With this opportunity to expand the new collection came the need for a planned program to acquire prints not only by artists in the United States but also by those in other parts of the world. But for this purpose copyright receipts were not helpful; as a matter of fact, they had ceased for some time to be a substantial source of prints of artistic interest. Through the 19th century prints of all kinds were normally deposited for copyright; but by the turn of the century, the flow had become largely one of prints intended for wide sale, as well as photographs and reproductions. This shift made it necessary then, as it does now, for the Library to rely on purchase funds and on gifts from sympathetic artists and collectors to increase its holdings of fine prints.

This effort has gone forward actively. The *Catalog of the Gardiner Greene Hubbard Collection of Engravings* was published by the Library of Congress in 1905. Subsequent chiefs of the Fine Arts Division, as it was then called, continued to organize the collections for use. Other gifts and acquisitions were received, notably the George Lothrop Bradley Collection, bequeathed in 1906 and received in 1919; the Charles L. Freer Collection; and the collection of Oliver Wendell Holmes, Jr., Associate Justice of the Supreme Court, acquired in 1953. The Hubbard, Bradley and Holmes' collections contain most of the "old master" prints; they provide an almost complete sequence, in impressions of varying quality, of the prints of Dürer and substantial holdings of the works of Rembrandt and of Jacques Callot.

A significant contribution to the collection of important modern prints came with the Pennell Collection and the Pennell Fund received in the 1930's. The Library's interest in fine printmaking had become more widely known in the 1920's through frequent public exhibitions, and the continuing work of building and organizing the collections. As a result, when Joseph Pennell, the American etcher and lithographer, returned to the United States from his years abroad he became interested in the Library's activities and a major benefactor of them. In addition to a fund for acquisitions, Mr. Pennell also left the Library a large selection of his own work and that of other artists, including an extensive collection of the work and papers of James McNeill Whistler. The Library received the collections and purchase fund in 1936.

Utilizing this endowment, a Committee to Select Prints for Purchase Under the Pennell Fund, composed of the chief of the Division of Prints and Photographs and two outstanding printmakers, recommends purchases of prints by both American and foreign artists, of the 19th and 20th centuries. The committee's selections have ranged broadly over the main aspects of contemporary printmaking, and have also increased the Library's holdings of works of the great 19th century masters such as Degas and Manet. The committee's work has been aided for three decades by the Library's sponsorship of the series of National Exhibitions of Prints. Cosponsored in 1973 with the Smithsonian's National Collection of Fine Arts, it is now a biennial event and has become a valuable public showcase both for the unknown printmaker and for the artist of established reputation, primarily those resident in the United States. Each exhibition is sent on tour to museums and cultural institutions after it closes in Washington.

Other American printmakers, such as George Bellows, John Sloan, Childe Hassam, and John Taylor Arms, or their families, have made gifts which, supplemented by purchases, have resulted in large holdings of their works. Many of these prints appear in *American Prints in the Library of Congress: A Catalog of the Collection,* compiled by Karen F. Beall and the staff of the Prints and Photographs Division and published for the Library of Congress by The Johns Hopkins Press (1970).

In addition to more than 75,000 artists' or fine prints, other resources of the division for the student of the fine arts include numerous master drawings, and sets of facsimiles of prints from major collections in Europe. Some prints of unusual quality and interest have been acquired through copyright deposit or as a part of larger gifts, but most have been obtained by the use of purchase funds which benefactors have provided or by other means of acquisition. To develop this resource, more common to a museum than a library, may seem strange in the context of the other pictures in this book. Yet works of art emphatically have a place in the Library of Congress. Just as in the book collections of the Library, works of poetry and drama are included along with treatises on economics, science, or history, so the pictorial collections comprise both the imaginative and the documentary.

186

[THE KNIGHT, DEATH, AND THE DEVIL] Engraving by Albrecht Dürer. 1513. Hubbard Collection.   LC-USZ62-17351

The embodiment of the Renaissance in the north of Europe, Dürer was interested in the sciences and the humanities, in the rediscovery of the antique and in modern developments, in philosophy and religion. A fine painter, but an even greater engraver, he created prints that are among the most important and influential of all time. His broad range of interests come together in the brilliant plate reproduced here, in which the extraordinary horse reflects a profound study of Italian Renaissance and Roman antique sculpture, the animal and plant forms suggest the detailed particularity of the natural scientist, and the juxtapositions of good and evil, beauty and ugliness, establish a powerful intellectual context. Scholars have long pondered the exact implication of the engraving, and there is no agreement on exactly what Dürer is saying here. Grimm, Panofsky, and others have connected this print with Erasmus's notion of the true Christian as a combatant against the flesh, the devil, and the world, and see the knight as a Christian soldier in a generalized sense; others have interpreted the print as referring to specific religious leaders, or to the forces of evil that attach themselves even to the good and the powerful.

187

[THE THREE TREES] Etching by Rembrandt Harmenszoon van Rijn. 1643. Hubbard Collection.
LC-USZ62-17353

No prints are more sought after today than those of Rembrandt, whose paintings and prints share a dramatic sense of atmosphere and mood created through the play of light. This quality is present with unparalleled force in his prints. Rembrandt combined the rich velvety black of the drypoint with the wiry and descriptive etched line in many of his prints, but rarely with more success than in this renowned landscape. The popularity of The Three Trees is such that at least nine printmakers since Rembrandt's time have etched copies of it.

188

[VILLAGE ON THE BANKS OF A RIVER] Etching by Antonio Canale, *called* Canaletto [Between 1741 and 1744] Hubbard Collection.

LC-USZ62-46598

In contrast to Rembrandt, the great Venetian landscape painter Canaletto capitalized upon the uniformity of line possible in etching. Some of his views were taken directly from nature, others have an element of invention or fantasy, but all have a lyric quality and shimmering light that appeal to the eye and entice the viewer into the picture. It is no wonder that Canaletto's prints as well as his paintings were popular with visiting Englishmen, in Italy on the fashionable grand tour, who wanted to take home a remembrance of their trip.

Il [Mondo] e [per] lo piu [Gabbia] di [Matti] Engraving by Giuseppe Maria Mitelli. 1684. Hubbard Fund.   LC-USZ62-46600

A fascinating artist of 17th-century Italy, Giuseppe Maria Mitelli of Bologna was a superb draftsman and engraver, and in effect, an early caricaturist giving his view of social and political conditions and the follies of human nature.

The print illustrated is titled in rebus form: "Il [mondo] e [per] lo piu [gabbia] di [matti]" —the world is, for the most part, a cage for madmen. In it one can find many breeds of men. Amusingly, near the top and outside the case, is the artist, undisturbed and absorbed with his palette and sketchbook. Below are gluttons, the assassin, the spendthrift, musicians, and merrymakers. The astronomer gazes at higher things; the old Jew has the "Cabala"—the Hebrew book of occult sciences. All presumably desire to reach the top, where Fortune sits dangling her bait.

Giorgio Nicodemi in a study of Mitelli attributes the quatrains at the bottom, a kind of annotation found in many of Mitelli's prints, to the artist. (In Achille Bertarelli, *Le Incisione di Giuseppe Maria Mitelli,* 1940, p. xxxiii) These lines state, in part, that "sooner or later everybody enters the cage" and that "in short, either in actions, or gestures, words or deeds, the world is mostly a cage of lunatics."

Mitelli was influenced by Annibale Carracci and made a set of 40 street cries inspired by those of Carracci, one of which follows.

190

[BOOK SELLER FROM THE *DIVERSE FIGURE*]
Etching by Simon Guillain after Annibale Carracci [1646]   LC-USZ62-42681

Before leaving his native Bologna in 1595 for Rome, the painter Annibale Carracci made 75 drawings of the street trades, which were bound into a book and used by students for their exercises in draftsmanship. In 1646, the young French artist Simon Guillain etched them (and five others by Carracci). This album, the *Diverse Figure,* became one of the most famous series of street cries ever made, and was reprinted in 1740 with minor changes. This print shows a vendor of books and tablets very much in motion on a street in Bologna, hoping to arrest the attention of a potential customer.

191

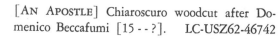

[An Apostle] Chiaroscuro woodcut after Domenico Beccafumi [15 - - ?]. LC-USZ62-46742

The 16th-century equivalent of today's best art reproductions was the chiaroscuro woodcut, which sought to imitate drawings with tonal effects created through the use of two or more blocks. It was, furthermore, an early means of introducing color into a printed image.

Beccafumi was well known as a painter and draftsman. A number of his woodcuts are among over 100 chiaroscuri in the Library's collections, most of which came from an album originally assembled by the Earl of Pembroke, and acquired by the Library in 1918.

192

[A Spanish Nobleman Places the Lance] Etching and aquatint by Francisco Goya y Lucientes [Between 1801-1813] Pennell Fund.
LC-USZ62-22044

A towering figure in the history of Spanish art, and one of the most imaginative printmakers of any nation, Goya is perhaps best known for his print cycles, *Los Proverbios, Los Disparates,* and *Los Desastres de la Guerra.* But he was also a keen student of the bull ring and—as seen in the print reproduced here—depicted this activity with vigor. The particular excitement of Goya's prints results in large measure from his massing of black, white, and grey areas through the use of the etching technique known as aquatint, as well as from his powerful command of the drawing of figures in action. This print is plate 34 in the third edition of *La Tauromachie,* published by E. Loizelet in Paris in 1876.

193

[AT THE PRADO] Aquatint by Édouard Manet [1865 or 1868] Pennell Fund.   LC-USZ62-46603

Primarily a painter, Manet was nevertheless among the first artists to revive the etching technique in France. Familiar with Goya's work in the medium, he used aquatint to establish dramatic effects of pattern in his prints, as in *At the Prado*. Contemporary life supplied most of Manet's subjects, in contrast to the artists of the previous generation in France.

194

[LEAVING FOR THE FIELDS] Etching by Jean François Millet (fifth state) [1863]
LC-USZ62-17354

Millet was a leader in the mid-19th century of a group of artists known as the Barbizon School, who resided in Barbizon at the forest of Fontainebleau. He depicts peaceful rural scenes in which peasants go about their daily chores in the fields bearing the weight of tools that, symbolically, seem to anchor them to the earth.

195

[NOCTURNE] Etching by James Abbott McNeill Whistler [1880] Hubbard Collection.

LC-USZ62-30998

Whistler, born in America, spent most of his life in Europe. Many subjects fascinated him —portraits (at which he was very successful), city scenes, interiors, and landscapes. *Nocturne,* published in 1880 as part of his Venice series, is an example of one of his landscape mood pieces. When making etchings, Whistler frequently took the plates with him rather than doing preliminary sketches from nature to be copied later on plates in the studio. The dark areas in sky and water on this print are the results of *retroussage*—that is, simply wiping ink onto these areas each time the plate is printed, instead of creating these effects with aquatint or etching.

196

[LE GRAND BASSIN—OSTEND] Etching by James Ensor [1888] Pennell Fund.   LC-USZ72-151

In striking contrast to Whistler's harbor scene, Ensor seems to animate ships, buildings, and water with a nervous movement transmitted by flicks, dashes, and spots. It is unusual to find this artist responding to a familiar scene without imbuing it with a quality of macabre fantasy, but in this print he seems content merely to suggest the active harbor scene at Ostend.

197

[DER WALCHENSEE] Drypoint by Lovis Corinth [1919] Pennell Fund.   LC-USZ62-46599

A virtuoso, particularly with drypoint, Corinth is as famous for his portraits and figure studies as for his landscapes, all of which display an energy of line few artists can match. His print of the Walchensee is more than just a view; it transmits the feeling of the artist's personal experience at this place. Corinth did in fact keep a small country house here in the Bavarian Alps, far from the pressures of the city.

198

THE GUARD GATE [GATUN LOCK] Lithograph by Joseph Pennell [1912] Pennell Collection.
LC-USZ62-3513

The Guard Gate at Gatun Lock is one of a series of lithographs made in 1912 during the construction of the Panama Canal, by the American printmaker Joseph Pennell. The artist always seemed able to select the best possible vantage point from which to sketch. He commented at the time: "I have never seen such a magnificent arrangement of line, light and mass, and yet those were the last things the engineers thought of. But great work is great art. . . . This is the Wonder of Work." (Louis A. Wuerth, *Catalogue of the Lithographs of Joseph Pennell,* 1931)

Lithography, invented in Germany just before 1800, was used by comparatively few artists during most of the 19th century, although it was a very significant medium for the printing of popular images, advertisements, and caricatures. Pennell was one of the leading advocates of its use by artists, starting in the 1890's, and many British and American printmakers worked in lithography as a result of reading his books and articles and seeing his prints. This print is from the nearly complete collection of his work which the artist gave to the Library of Congress.

199

[SELF-PORTRAIT] Woodcut by Erich Heckel [1917] Pennell Fund.   LC-USZ72-68

Shortly after the turn of the century, when the expressionist movement started in Germany, artists associated with it revolted against academic traditions and rejected the passionless decorative styles of the 1890's in favor of a direct, intense, emotional statement. In Munich, the *Blaue Reiter* group sought nonfigurative equivalents for feelings and action, while in Dresden *Die Brücke* consisted of figurative expressionists. Heckel belonged to this latter group. The self-portrait was made in 1917 quite early in the artist's career. Heckel and his colleagues particularly favored bold forms and slashing knife cuts of the woodblock. Along with Paul Gauguin and Edvard Munch they gave a new vitality to this most ancient graphic medium.

200

[THE ENGRAVER JOSEPH TOURNY] Etching by Edgar Degas [1857] Pennell Fund.

LC-USZ62-22051

This almost classical portrait differs markedly from the preceding expressionist one and from that which follows. The subject of this print, Joseph Tourny, may have taught Degas the art of etching during a trip by the latter to Rome in 1856. This was still very much within Degas' formative years—he was 21 at the time—yet the etching shows the skill of a master draftsman. The controlled contours of the figure (a hallmark of Degas' style) obscure the connection of this composition with Rembrandt's famous etched self-portrait at an open window. As a student of etching, Degas devoted himself to intensive study of the greatest master of the medium.

The little studies of clerics' heads below the lower margin of this early version of the composition were effaced in later prints. The artist probably took advantage of an available bit of plate to record an attractive subject, never intending to retain his sketch except in an early proof of the print.

201

JOHN BROWN. Lithograph by Charles W. White. 1949. Pennell Fund.   LC-USZ62-46932

White's powerful images convey a strong sense of life and of experience with the subjects depicted. He is a major interpreter of black citizens in the variety of their roles in and their contributions to American life. His approach and style have been strongly influenced by his student ties with artists of social realism in Mexico, where he learned the art of lithography.

Upon completion of his art education he worked on art projects with the Works Progress Administration in the 1930's. He has enjoyed some 30 years of recognition in his profession, as indicated, in part, by the numerous fellowships and other awards he has won. He is a painter as well as printmaker and has been a college teacher and lecturer. His illustrations appear in a number of books, and his works are in major galleries and private collections.

205

202

W[HITE] L[INE] S[QUARE] VIII. Lithograph by Josef Albers [19]66. Pennell Fund.

LC-USZ62-46743

and   **203**

[SELF-PORTRAIT] Lithograph by Josef Albers [1916-1918] Gift and Pennell Fund.

LC-USZ62-43078

Shown are two prints, both lithographs, done by German-born Josef Albers some 50 years apart. Albers was both a student and a master at the famous Bauhaus in Germany—the center of the European avant-garde during the 1920's and early 1930's. The primary aim of the Bauhaus was to try to bring together art and technology in order to create artistic objects with the potential for mass production, and to do this a special attitude toward the elements of design was developed. *White Line Square* belongs to the familiar series *Homage to the Square* (both painted and printed) in which Albers investigates the changing effects of tonal values and colors when juxtaposed.

In *White Line Square* every trace of "hand work" is effaced, to focus our concentration on the planes and shapes of the composition. In Albers' remarkable *Self-Portrait* the sense of structure is no less evident but it is coupled with an intense revelation of the play of light on solid shapes. In addition to its significance as a record of the physical appearance and psychology of the artist, the *Self-Portrait* is a milestone along the road from the spatial conceptualization of Cézanne, and the cubist style of Picasso, Braque and Juan Gris, to the complete nonobjectivity of subsequent decades.

204

[DELMONICO BUILDING] Lithograph by Charles Sheeler. 1927. Pennell Fund.   LC-USZ62-46601

Images of Philadelphia-born Charles Sheeler, photographer, painter, and printmaker, display clarity and harmony through the use of simple planes and volumes. His scenes from the American environment are often quite specific, as in this lithograph of the Delmonico Building, but in other cases his precisionist vision revealed highly abstract composition in the architecture, machinery, and furniture of which he was so fond. The sloping planes in perspective and the exact observation of light and shade show how Sheeler's eye was guided by his interest in photography.

205

UNDERSEA. Engraving by Stanley William Hayter
[19]37. Pennell Fund.   LC-USZ62-43291

Few printmaker-teachers of this century rank
in importance with Stanley William Hayter. His
Atélier 17 (located at different times in Paris
and New York) has had worldwide influence for
close to half a century, particularly in terms of
technical innovations in relief and color etching.
Hayter derived his imagery directly from the
linear rhythms inherent in the physical act of
engraving on metal. He then developed these
rhythms further on the basis of the way he perceived them. Hayter's esthetic position grew out
of his association with the surrealists in Paris and
his familiarity with their notion of the creative
force of the unconscious and the subconscious.

Countless outstanding artists working today
began as students of Hayter, including Mauricio
Lasansky and Gabor Peterdi.

210

206

ANGRY GULF. Drypoint by Gabor Peterdi. 1971. Pennell Fund.	LC-USZ62-41625

One of Hayter's most admired students is Gabor Peterdi, now a professor at Yale University and an artist of exceptional skill. This skill can be seen in *Angry Gulf,* in the suggestion of the forces of nature embodied in the violent action of ocean or flood waters. The technical excellence and strength of his images are extraordinary. He is an energetic and perceptive artist with a deep understanding of the history of art, and he serves as a member of the Library's Pennell Committee.

207

[SUBURBAN] Lithograph by Robert Rauschenberg. 1962. Pennell Fund.   LC-USZ62-46604

Robert Rauschenberg creates some sense of contemporary turmoil in pictorial terms. The print illustrated is the lithographic equivalent of a collage, combining photomechanical reproductions of old pictures (in this case, a house, chair, and a train wreck) with freely drawn brushwork. Rauschenberg was one of a well-known group of artists in the 1960's who made much use of the process of transferring printed images from discarded printing plates, with solvents or by photosilkscreens, onto stones for conventional lithographic printing, thus exploring new imagery in a traditional technique.

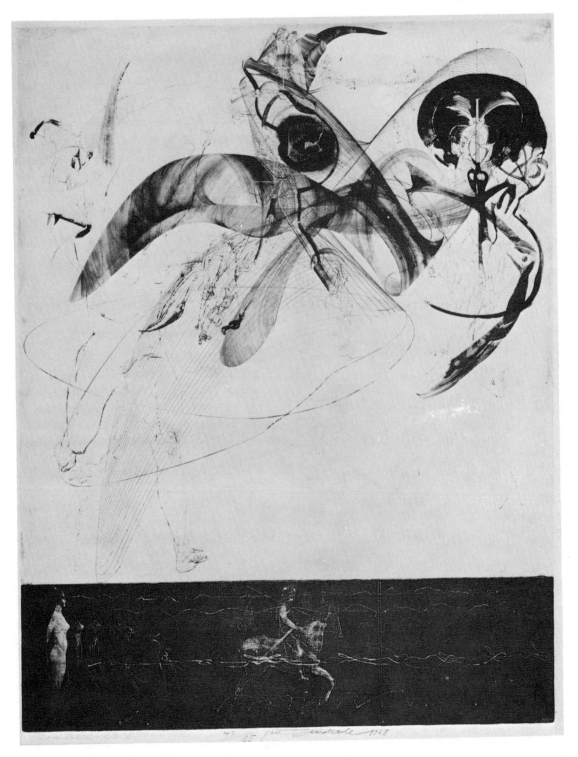

208

COMÉDIE No. 6. Etching and engraving by Jiří Anderle. 1968. Pennell Fund.   LC-USZ62-46602

Another artist who combines abstract and figurative elements, but with a totally different effect than Rauschenberg, is the Czech, Jiří Anderle, whose technical mastery and complex imagery are arresting.

An etcher, lithographer, and actor, Anderle often borrows literary themes for his prints, as is the case with *Comédie No. 6* from Dante. Literary references and social and political connotations underlie the prints of many Czechoslovakian graphic artists. Since the early 1960's some of the most impressive prints have come from them.

209

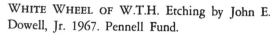

WHITE WHEEL OF W.T.H. Etching by John E. Dowell, Jr. 1967. Pennell Fund.

LC-USZ62-35498

"White Wheel of W[est] T[erre] H[aute]" was shown in the 1969 National Exhibition of Prints sponsored by the Library of Congress and was purchased for the permanent collections. Both an imaginative artist and a skillful technician, Dowell is a leading printmaker in the United States today. Formerly an assistant professor of art at the University of Illinois, he went to Rome in 1971 to join the overseas faculty of the Tyler School of Art, Temple University.

210

[COMPOSITION] Serigraph by Miroslav Sutej [1967] Pennell Fund. LC-USZ62-46744

Since 1955 a biennial print exhibition initiated by Zoran Kržišnik has been held in Ljubljana, Yugoslavia, a traditional art center. This has provided impetus and exposure for graphic artists of all countries and has been a stimulating force for Yugoslavs. One of these is Miroslav Sutej, who was born in Kutina and studied in Zagreb.

Josef Albers used the repetition of a single form of varying value (see *White Line Square*) to turn optical phenomena into pure aesthetic objects in his pictures. Sutej creates visual effects of distortion, producing bulges in some areas and affecting the entire image by depicting passage through planes and space. The very process of transformation is clear and adds to the dramatic sense of the print.

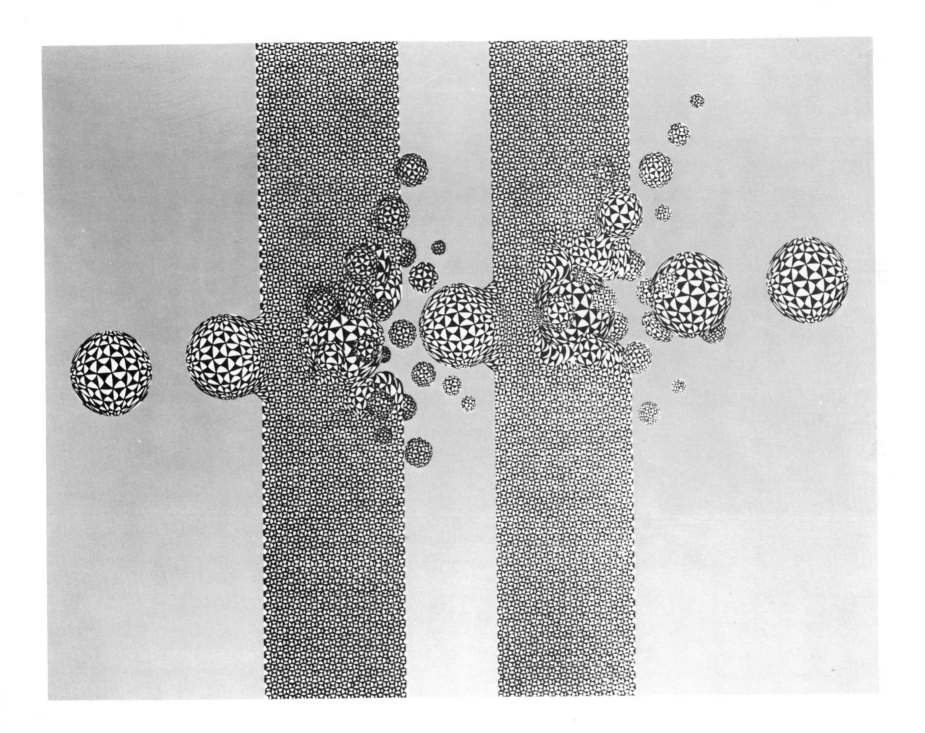

215

Index

Numbers in italic type refer to page numbers; the others refer to entries. Titles of prints appear, with some abbreviation, as given in the captions.

☆ U.S. GOVERNMENT PRINTING OFFICE: 1974 O—470-879